The Little Black Book: on Narcissists

By Miss Anonymous

Library of Congress Cataloging-in-Publication Data
Names: Anonymous, Miss, author.

Title: The Little Black Book / Miss Anonymous
Description: Los Angeles, California : Miss Anonymous | Includes bibliographical references and index.

Identifiers: ASIN B08GK2BZWH (e-book) ISBN 9798679169029 (pbk. : alk.paper) | Subjects: LCSH: Narcissism. | Interpersonal relations.

Table of Contents

Survivor of abuse, who wishes to remain anonymous has created the ideal manual on narcissists by blending citations from psychiatrists, psychologists, professors, scientists, research studies, etc. to validate everyone's experiences with the narcissists in their life. This book saves lives !!

The Author has accomplished this by creating a virtual bible on the devil. The perfect reference guide in understanding narcissists in the easiest way possible.

The ideal purse companion for every lady.
The ideal pocket buddy for every man.
This book delivers in spades, as displayed throughout this well-researched masterpiece.

Introduction

There are people in this world who are natural born hunters, preying on those with rich, empathetic qualities. Those with strong feelings and emotions with an authentic sense of self are perfect targets for these predators, otherwise known as narcissists.

According to *Psychology Today*, "The hallmarks of Narcissistic Personality Disorder (NPD) are grandiosity, a lack of empathy for other people, and a need for admiration. People with this condition are frequently described as arrogant, self-centered, manipulative, and demanding."[1]

According to the Diagnostic and Statistical Manual of Mental Disorders (DSM-5), NPD is defined as comprising a pervasive pattern of grandiosity (in fantasy or behavior), a constant need for admiration, and a lack of empathy, beginning by early adulthood and present in a variety of contexts, as indicated by the presence of at least five of the following nine criteria:

1. A grandiose sense of self-importance (e.g., the individual exaggerates achievements and talents and expects to be recognized as superior without commensurate achievements);

2. A preoccupation with fantasies of unlimited success, power, brilliance, beauty, or ideal love;

3. A belief that they are special and unique and can only be understood by, or should associate with, other special or high-status people or institutions;

4. A need for excessive admiration;

5. A sense of entitlement (i.e., unreasonable expectations of especially favorable treatment or automatic compliance with their expectations);

6. Interpersonally exploitive behavior (i.e., the individual takes advantage of others to achieve his or her own ends);

---

[1] "Narcissistic Personality Disorder." *Psychology Today*, Sussex Publishers, 2018, www.psychologytoday.com/us/conditions/narcissistic-personality-disorder.

7. A lack of empathy (unwillingness to recognize or identify with the feelings and needs of others);
8. Envy of others or a belief that others are envious of them;
9. A demonstration of arrogant and haughty behaviors or attitudes[2].

The defining factor with every narcissist is a complete disconnect from conscience resulting in a total lack of empathy. Narcissists cannot feel remorse; instead, they receive pleasure from hurting others. Those who have empathy cannot possibly be a narcissist.

Narcissists have only the cruelest intentions and typically place themselves in positions of power — lawyer, doctor, government, clergy, administration, CEO, business owner — so they can exercise their superiority over others and the abuse of power can begin. Some victims become completely dependent on the narcissist for their very survival. Narcissists use this to their advantage as they manipulate everyone, fooling even those closest to them, while their ulterior motives go undetected. They feed their victim a stream of lies and expect it to be embraced as reality; the victim mixes the narcissist's lies with their own reality. A stream of false accusations is presented, which wears down the victim over time and sparks some intense emotional reactions. Victims are left trying to make sense of it all while they are constantly on guard, trying to defend something that does not exist. The narcissist wants the victim to appear crazy and unstable and will use their emotional outburst to back up this claim.

People believe if a person takes too many selfies, they are a narcissist, and this could not be further from the truth. Everyone has some level of narcissism, and this alone does not define someone as a narcissist. Narcissism is only one of three aspects that contribute to every narcissist's dark way of thinking. The other two traits are psychopathy, where genetics and brain chemistry mix with environmental factors to contribute to the development of psychopathic traits, and Machiavellianism, which is characterized as a person who manipulates and exploits others to suit their purpose.[3]

---

[2] Ambardar, Sheenie. "What Are the DSM-5 Diagnostic Criteria for Narcissistic Personality Disorder (NPD)?" *Latest Medical News, Clinical Trials, Guidelines – Today on Medscape*, 16 July 2018, www.medscape.com/answers/1519417-101773/what-are-the-dsm-5-diagnostic-criteria-for-narcissistic-personality-disorder-npd.

[3] Whitbourne, Susan Krauss. "Shedding Light on Psychology's Dark Triad." *Psychology Today*, Sussex Publishers, 2013, www.psychologytoday.com/ca/blog/fulfillment-any-age/201301/shedding-light-psychology-s-dark-triad.

These characteristics enable narcissists to live life carte blanche, giving them the freedom to treat people as possessions. People are mere objects to be manipulated and controlled within the confines of a delusional mind. They feel their cruel behavior is justified and that people deserve what they get.

One tactic that narcissist use is gaslighting or creating an illusionary truth. Preston Ni, M.S.B.A., a writer for *Psychology Today*, suggests gaslighting is a form of persistent manipulation and brainwashing that causes the victim to doubt her or himself. Ultimately, it leads to a loss of one's own sense of perception, identity, and self-worth. A gaslighter's statements and accusations are often based on deliberate falsehoods and calculated marginalization.[4]

Involvement with a narcissist is like riding a merry-go-round: the narcissist spins the wheel of abuse, and as the momentum and speed the abuse pick up, the victim becomes confused, inevitably leading to pure exhaustion. It seems like a never-ending ride while the victim is on it, but when the ride does finally come to a stop, it can be just as dangerous for the victim.

The interpersonal relations that started as an intense, intriguing connection will erupt into a firestorm when the victim starts realizing what is happening and attempts to confront the narcissist. Some leave, and others stay; of these victims, some are even are murdered. Statistics from the U.S. Department of Justice indicate that Intimate partner violence accounts for 15 percent of all violent crime.[5]

 It is important to remember just how dangerous narcissists really are and are not to be taken lightly. First let us start by finding out how the predator, also known as the narcissist, finds their prey and how all this begins.

---

[4] Ni, Preston. "6 Common Traits of Narcissists and Gaslighters." *Psychology Today*, Sussex Publishers, 2017, www.psychologytoday.com/ca/blog/communication-success/201707/6-common-traits-narcissists-and-gaslighters.
[5] Truman, Jennifer L. "Nonfatal Domestic Violence 2003-2012." *Bureau of Justice Statistics,* US Department of Justice, 2013, www.bjs.gov/content/pub/pdf/ndv0312.pdf.

Chapter 1
Predator on the Hunt

A narcissist, by nature, is a predator, and is always on the prowl looking for new prey. Their thinking patterns are primal, so they relate much of what they do to nature as they consider people objects to stalk, hunt, and lure into a well-orchestrated trap. Once caught, the narcissist will move in for the kill in the ultimate psychological game of manipulation, dominance, power, and control.

To find the perfect target, the narcissist must first go on the hunt. Perhaps it could be the person they noticed in the car beside them and decided to follow home or someone they found online. Once their curiosity is piqued and someone has caught their interest, it is game on. Time to zero in and begin stalking to learn more.

The narcissist is now hiding in the background of the victim's life and observing every single move that makes their prey predictable. Every detail is meticulously stored within the hollows of a delusional mind, which will eventually be used to capture, keep, and destroy their prey.

A National Intimate Partner and Sexual Violence Survey conducted by the National Center for Injury Prevention and Control (CDC) reveals that one in seven women and one in 18 men have been stalked by an intimate partner during their lifetime, frequently to the point in which they felt very fearful or believed that they or someone close to them would be harmed or killed.[6]

A new obsession is born: watching in person and/or online, the narcissist begins to learn every single detail about the victim, including their family and friends, their career and religion, any habits, traits, and values, likes and dislikes, and so on. No predator likes to be caught off guard, so the narcissist must know their prey as well as they know themselves.

The narcissist begins to develop a mirrored persona by emulating the target to appear as if they have everything in common. A new mask of deceit and deception is exquisitely crafted. Narcissists need to move quickly to make sure their ulterior motives and their real self-remain securely hidden. The narcissist must be certain they cannot fail before they will proceed; they will wait until the timing is exactly right to strike.

---

[6] Black, Michele C. "National Intimate Partner and Sexual Violence Survey." NISVS, 2011, www.cdc.gov/violenceprevention/pdf/nisvs_report2010-a.pdf.

Once the narcissist is prepared, they will either make first contact or maneuver the circumstances so that the victim approaches them. Either way, the victim is doomed to be fooled by the crafty narcissist who is only interested in possessing them, not getting to know them. The narcissist already knows the victim way too well from studying them ahead of time, but the unsuspecting target believes they just met.

Every move has been planned and anticipated to ensure their initial approach and subsequent communication will not fail. The narcissist wants to gain instant trust; after all, first impressions are vital, and the cunning narcissist knows this is the most important step.

The initial approach is surprising for most victims, as they are taken aback by how fast they are being showered with praise, adoration, and gestures of love. The goal is to draw prey in quickly, which they accomplish by creating the illusion of trust, loyalty, love, intimacy, and affection, all designed to captivate the victim while their ulterior motives go undetected. The narcissist is only looking to capture the victim's love, not return it.

While dining in a restaurant with a menu of love, the empathetic victim sees compassion, empathy, care, and authenticity. The narcissist, looking at the same menu, sees hate, lies, control, dominance, and cruel intentions, with their new victim as the main entree to whet their appetite.

Chapter 2

Empath Versus Narcissist

Narcissists are highly attracted to empathetic people, otherwise known as "empaths," so that is whom they target. Just as narcissistic men are drawn to empathetic women, so are narcissistic women drawn to empathetic men. Abuse does not discriminate and can happen in any interpersonal relationship between two people from any walk of life.

According to the Oxford English Dictionary, empathy is defined as the ability to understand and share in the feelings of another.[7] Empaths are drenched with care and compassion while riddled with natural expression and emotion. Empaths possess the unique ability to feel someone else's emotions. These traits make all empaths vulnerable to narcissistic predators.

Self-proclaimed narcissist HD Tudor claims, "Empaths are always targeted as primary sources and it's those empathetic traits that lead all empaths to be ensnared and heavily exploited by narcissists."[8]

Like a moth drawn to a flame, the unsuspecting victim, the empathy, doesn't realize the danger hidden behind what appears the perfect person who gives them everything they want, saying all the right things, sweeping them off their feet, and making them feel so special. If these intentions were true, then this would be great. But that is not the case with narcissists, as their intentions are always deceiving.

Narcissist HG Tudor freely admits:

> The false strength which the narcissist exhibits at the outset of the seduction, the confidence, the apparent satisfaction with his self, that he appears comfortable in his own skin, at ease with others, capable of lighting up a room and so forth is a huge attraction to the Empath

---

[7] "Empathy | Definition of Empathy in English by Oxford Dictionaries." *Oxford Dictionaries | English*, Oxford Dictionaries, 2014, en.oxforddictionaries.com/definition/empathy.

[8] Sutton, Debra. "Sins of the Empath: Truth Seeker by Narcissist H.G. Tudor." *Signs of a Gay Husband* by Debra Sutton, 1 Oct. 2017, signsofagayhusbandbydebrasutton.wordpress.com/2017/10/01/sins-of-the-empath-truth-seeker-by-narcissist-h-g-tudor/comment-page-1/#comment-2223.

because that person actually sees something of themselves in the narcissist when the narcissist is seducing.[9]

The Illusion of a Twin Flame

The narcissist emulates the empath's needs, wants, and desires and can manufacture the illusion of a soul mate. The trusting empath begins opening and shares every feeling, thought, and life experience; an intimate bond begins to form. The empath slowly becomes convinced they have finally discovered their perfect soul mate, their twin flame.

Mateo Sol, a prominent psycho-spiritual teacher whose work has influenced the lives of thousands of people worldwide defines a twin flame to be: a person who you feel connected to not just on a physical and emotional level, but also on a soulful or spiritual level.10

Masking themselves as the empath's twin flame, the narcissist puts on a good act and captures the empath's undivided attention. Narcissist HG Tudor states that narcissists show the empath all they want to see by mirroring them. This gives the empath all the comforts they are looking for, but they are being lied to and manipulated.11

The empath now feels they have connected with the narcissist on a deeper level. The narcissist plays on the empath's emotions, with stories of woe that cause the empath to sympathize with the wounded narcissist. Empaths will instinctually shower the narcissist will love and affection, trying to fix all the broken pieces.

The Difference Between Sympathy and Empathy

Too often people confuse empathy and sympathy. Empathy is "the ability to understand and share the feelings of another, whereas sympathy is to 'feel pity and sorrow for someone else's misfortune.'"[12]

Narcissists tell stories of woe, which tug at the empath's heart strings and cause them to feel sorrow for the poor narcissist's misfortune. Internally, the empath is not able to relate to the narcissist's feelings because they are an act

[9] Tudor, HG. "The Super Empath." *Knowing the Narcissist*, 22 May 2018, narcsite.com/2018/05/23/the-super-empath-8/comment-page-1/.
[10] Sol, Mateo. "Twin Flame: Your Guide to Experiencing Rare Transcendental Love" LonerWolf, 10 Oct. 2018, lonerwolf.com/twin-flame/.
[11] Sutton, 2017.
[12] Oxford, 2014.

to gain attention; the expressions of the narcissist don't have the emotions to back them up.

Narcissists are missing that vital connection to their own soulful energy, whereas empaths have a strong connection to theirs. From that vital energy, beautiful character traits bloom such as:

Compassion

Empaths feel deeply for every living thing. They want to pour their love onto others any chance they get. Love exudes them, and all they touch benefit from their tender heart. Tender loving care is at the heart of every empath and in a healthy relationship this quality is amazing, but in a toxic relationship with a narcissist, an empath's compassion will be the target of destruction.

An empath cannot stop caring, so once they develop feelings of care for a narcissist it is hard to just flip a switch and turn them off. Empaths have an incredible ability to love even those who do them the most wrong, because their care runs that deep.

Integrity

Narcissists feel no remorse for harming their victims, whereas their victims are apprehensive about retaliating or turning their back on the narcissist. Normally this quality is terrific in a healthy relationship, however not in an abusive relationship where this keeps victims viciously bonded when they should be walking away. A person's integrity becomes a weapon of choice used against them to destroy their very sense of self and trust in all that is around them.

Resilience

Highly resilient people are unlikely to give up on the narcissist, even after periods of abuse, even though they have an enhanced ability to detect a threatening environment. They will ignore their instincts, which are literally screaming at them, and fight for the toxic relationship, adopting a savior/fighter mentality as they attempt to sustain an unsustainable relationship. Some empaths measure their love by the amount of cruelty they can withstand.

Sentimental nature

A narcissist enjoys creating pleasurable memories they know the empath will romanticize about during the abusive periods of the relationship. Sentimental people wear their heart on their sleeve and forgive easily, which the narcissist manipulates with ease.

Charisma

Empaths have a vibrant soul, so they are very articulate when communicating and their energy is electric. They can light up a room just by walking into it. They have that way of carrying themselves and expressing themselves. This is what angers the narcissist the most, as they look to shut all that down and break the empath's spirit. They do this because they cannot experience these sensations and are jealous of those who can.

Despite the cruel treatment of a narcissist, empaths can use the wonderful qualities they possess to detach themselves from the narcissist. They can accomplish this by using their natural empathy to practice compassion on themselves. Nobody deserves to be mistreated, and everyone is worthy of a relationship that is healthy, loving, and grows naturally.

Even though the narcissist may appear sincere, they are really hiding their true self under a mask of deception. They want to appear as though they have the same wonderful traits as an empath, but the truth is they do not. They hide their true self under a mask of deception because if people knew the narcissists true self, they would run for the hills. There are monumental differences between the empath and narcissist as these two forces are stellar opposite to one another.

The empath, who is only looking for honesty and love, meets the ultimate deception when they come face to face with a narcissist. The toxic connection between these two forces is explosive as the narcissist manipulates the empath's feelings and emotions.

Now that we have taken a close look at the empath and understand they are prey for narcissists, let us take an in-depth look into the mind of a narcissist to better understand why they function the way they do.

The Empath	The Narcissist
Experiences remorse and guilt	Does not feel remorse or guilt
Has a strong connection to conscience	Has a complete disconnect to conscience
Raw feelings and emotions flow while bringing all that is natural and good to the world	Superficial charm masks a deeply rooted distain for the world
Receives pleasure by giving and receiving love	Receives pleasure by causing pain and suffering
Strong feelings of remorse when they make mistakes	Accountable for nothing, believing they make no mistakes
Rarely hold a grudge and are quick to forgive	Hold grudges and always seek revenge
Feel compassion and sorrow when seeing someone suffer	Cannot relate with those suffering and instead experience feelings of indifference
Naive at heart, does not know the first thing about manipulating people	An expert in the art of controlling, dominating and manipulating people
Possess a rich, vital energy supply that contributes to a positive flow in humanity	Depletes rich, vital energy supplies from all humanity
Full of expression and body language matching emotions	Limited in natural expression and rarely do words match body language
Avoids conflict	Creates conflict

Gaslighting - No More Secrets - Taking Off the Mask

Chapter 3

A Peek Inside the Mind of a Narcissistic Gaslighter

Narcissists believe it is disrespectful when you do not allow them to disrespect you. A narcissist views those who try and stand up to their abusive tactics as defiant, in need of punishment.

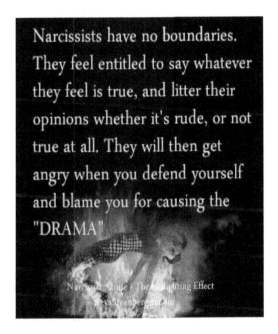

Narcissists have no boundaries. They feel entitled to say whatever they feel is true, and litter their opinions whether it's rude, or not true at all. They will then get angry when you defend yourself and blame you for causing the "DRAMA"

N ~ Narcissistic Personality Disorder
A ~ Avoids Accountability
R ~ Rages childishly and covertly
C ~ Controlling as a way of asserting Their superiority
I ~ Instills doubt
S ~ Stonewalls during conflicts
S ~ Smears and slanders
I ~ Integrates and gaslights
S ~ Silent treatment
T ~ Triangulates

Locked deep within the dark triad of their mind, a narcissist has three distinct character traits that contribute to the behavior associated with narcissistic personality disorder.

- Narcissism: one's obsessive need for vanity, self-love, self-admiration, and self-centeredness; the world revolves around them.

- Machiavellianism: characterized as a person who manipulates and exploits others to suit their purpose; bitingly cold, cruel, and unfeeling.

- Psychopathy: genetics and brain anatomy mixed with environmental factors contribute to the development of psychopathic traits.

According to Jared DeFife Ph.D., a writer for *Psychology Today*, the definition of what a personality disorder is now different than it was in the past: "instead of a pervasive pattern of thinking/emotionality/behaving, a personality disorder reflects adaptive failure involving impaired sense of self-identity or failure to develop effective interpersonal functioning."[13]

If a person has at least five or more of the following traits, this indicates they have narcissistic personality disorder, according to the DSM-5 (The *Diagnostic and Statistical Manual of Mental Disorders (DSM–5)*.[14]

1) Possesses a grandiose sense of self-importance by exaggerating their achievements and skills as to achieve recognition they are unworthy of

2) Believe they are a superior human being who is gifted and should be admired for their brilliant self

3) Preoccupied with visions of insurmountable success and possessions such as luxury property, sports cars, designer clothing, etc.

4) Exploits and flaunts the flaws in others while assuming no accountability f or theirs

5) Cannot relate to the feelings of others due to a disconnect from conscience resulting in a loss of authenticity

6) Are extremely envious of others while believing everyone is envious of them.

7) Haughty, arrogant, egocentric behavior and attitude

A narcissist is defined by a history of abnormal behavior that is identified by exaggerated feelings of self-importance and a need for excessive attention and admiration. Narcissists lack the ability to understand, to empathize, with the feelings of others. They never accept responsibility for their actions and

---

[13] DeFife, Jared. "DSM-V Offers New Criteria for Personality Disorders." *Psychology Today*, Sussex Publishers, 2010, www.psychologytoday.com/us/blog/the-shrink-tank/201002/dsm-v-offers-new-criteria-personality-disorders.
[14] Ambardar, 2018.

choices and are notorious for casting blame on others for their failures in life.

Not all narcissists are the same. According to Alethia Luna, spiritual writer and co-owner of Loner Wolf, most narcissists can be lumped into two main categories: vulnerable narcissists and invulnerable narcissists.[15]

Vulnerable Narcissists (VN)

Childhood abuse produces an inferiority complex, which fuels feelings of unworthiness and low self-esteem in the abused. To compensate as adults, vulnerable narcissists hide behind a grandiose mask of self-importance, lacking the ability to genuinely experience love. VNs use emotional manipulation such as gaslighting, guilt-tripping, and shaming to control and manipulate others.

Invulnerable Narcissists (IN)

This is the typical narcissist who lives with a complete disconnect from their conscience. They are thick-skinned and shamelessly seek power, glory, recognition, and pleasure.

Alethia Luna also believes that the two main types of narcissists can be broken down into four different subtypes: the amorous narcissist, the compensatory narcissist, the elite narcissist, and the malignant narcissist. Certain traits may overlap from subtype to subtype.[16]

The Amorous Narcissist

The Casanova of narcissists is driven by sexual desire. These deviant narcissists operate to control others to satisfy their sexual appetite. Once bored and the supply runs out, they will discard their victims quickly to find replacements, going through partners rapidly. Flaunting porn and sexual innuendoes, these narcissists are sex addicts with no moral conscience whatsoever. They view people as objects to sexually disrespect and use, leaving behind many broken hearts along the way.

---

[15] Luna, Aletheia, et al. "Dear Empaths: 4 Types of Narcissists You May Be Attracting LonerWolf." LonerWolf, 1 Oct. 2018, lonerwolf.com/empaths-and-narcissists/.

[16] Luna, 2018.

The Compensatory Narcissist

These narcissists seek those who are emotionally vulnerable. They are masters at setting up false presentations, painting themselves to be big and powerful,   masking insecurities and a deeply rooted fear criticism. They want people who
will serve as a pawn on their chessboard of manipulation and control. The compensatory narcissist loves to emotionally abuse others.

The Elite Narcissist

Highly dominant and power hungry, these narcissists believe they are a superior form of human being that should be praised and honored for everything they do. Their overwhelming sense of entitlement contaminates every area of their life, from relationships and friendships to finances. They are the biggest self-promoters and will stop at nothing to reach the top, no matter how many people they step on along the way. These narcissists typically find themselves in positions of power without taking the traditional route to get there (formal education).

The Malignant Narcissist

Haughty and arrogant, the malignant narcissist loves to outsmart people with a total lack of remorse or sadness for their immoral actions. They will never be held accountable and typically embark in criminal behavior. This type of narcissist is most likely to become involved in fraud schemes.

Narcissists all have one thing in common and that is their thinking pattern. They might fool you into believing they respect and love you but underneath the mask of deception they view empathetic people in a completely different light. To a narcissist, emotions are considered a sign of weakness, and therefore cast a negative light on those driven by instinct. Here is how a narcissist really views others.

INSIDE THE MIND OF A NARCISSISTIC PERSONALITY

HOW THEY VIEW THEMSELVES		HOW THEY VIEW YOU	
	Blameless		Guilty
	Victorious		Defeated
	Superior		Inferior
	Correct		Wrong
	Harmed		Hurtful
	Victimized		Attacker
	Intelligent		Stupid
	Exemplary		Unworthy
	Perfect		Flawed
	Balanced		Psycho
	Peacemaker		Instigator
	Truthful		Liar
	Happy		Angry
	Hard Worker		Lazy
	Popular		Hated
	Lucid		Delusional

Narcissist Abuse - The Gaslighting Effect
Author: Reva Steenbergen

The Behavior of a Narcissist

Narcissists have a sense of superiority over others. For example, they are overly critical and judgmental about others, possessing a haughty persona with grandiose displays of arrogance to cover up their deeply rooted insecurities.

Narcissists will always gravitate toward positions that will allow them to exercise control over others and manipulate those who are underneath them. Positions of power — lawyer, doctor, politician, military leader — grant these opportunities, whereas they steer clear of jobs such as factory or restaurant workers.

They have a sense of entitlement that sometimes comes off as confidence that manifests itself in a "carte blanche" attitude; they feel the world is one blank check to which they can fill in any amount. Everything is a free-for-all and nothing is off limits. They feel the world revolves around them, has done them terrible wrong, and owes them something, which they collect from people through abuse.

Romantic relationships move quickly, so the narcissist's ulterior motives remain undetected. Narcissists shower victims with adoration and over-the-top affection to get the victim hooked on their "fake love" supply. The narcissist is looking to create an intimate bond, so the victim's feelings of love can be used to control them in unspeakable ways.

Once they have the victim's interest, the narcissist may begin to subtly ignore them, appearing to lose interest or get distracted; perhaps they frequently check their phone while in a conversation. This is designed to pique curiosity and keep the victim interested by creating the illusion they are wanted, desired, and in high demand. This falsehood keeps the victim hooked, as they believe the narcissist is an important person whose attention needs to be fought for.

Narcissists always try and hold others accountable for their deceitful actions. They believe they are too perfect to be flawed and instead use the victim's flaws to paint them under a bad light. Thus, they exploit the very essence of who they are whilst promoting themselves as a good, well-balanced person. A narcissist cannot bear shame, so they project that shame onto others.

Narcissists have two sets of rules: those that apply to them and those that apply to everyone else. They may have unrealistic expectations of love and nurturing from others but do not hold themselves to the same high standards. They want you to adore, love, and praise them, to hold them at the highest level of respect while they walk all over your personal boundaries and have no idea how to genuinely love someone.

Narcissists view personal boundaries as a barricade to be blown up as they walk over the charred debris, forging themselves straight into the victim's "personal space", where, in essence, they try to make the victim understand they are not allowed rights or basic freedom.

The only time a narcissist performs a "good deed" is when they are looking for recognition or something in return. For example, acts of kindness allow them to fake empathy by showing others how giving they are and how helpful toward their fellow man. Or perhaps they will be helpful if they are looking for something in return that they will collect on down the road. Everyone is simply an object to be used and manipulated within the confines of their delusional mind.

They have a my-way-or-the-highway attitude. They believe that they know best that their way of doing things is the correct way, and any opposition is met with great distain and considered "narcissistic injury." Once someone disagrees with a narcissist, the abuse starts rolling, as they feel slighted and start to punish the victim. They may be overly sensitive to criticism or any suggestion that they are not in the right, which can provoke arguments and assertions of "you started it."

The more ruthless, cunning, disgusting, malicious, and contemptuous a narcissist can be, the more pleased they are. Their cruelty has no boundaries, and once a boundary is crossed, the narcissist looks to break down all boundaries until there is none left standing in their way. A narcissist believes their cruel treatment is always justified because the victim deserved it.

Narcissists thrive off chaos, strife, and drama, so they create this atmosphere as often as possible by creating long-winded rounds of nonsensical arguments that travel in a circular motion, leaving the victim questioning how it all started in the first place. The victim simply disagreed with the narcissist's claim the sky is green and now their whole life is under scrutiny and attack.

Narcissists refuse to be held accountable; therefore, the victim's feelings are always met with confrontation. Feelings are never validated, leaving victims with an overwhelming lack of resolve.

With every narcissist comes an anti-social personality that causes them to misread normal body language and logical human signals. Everyone is moving in one direction and the narcissist in the other. The narcissistic personality disorder that steers their behavior causes them to function in a way that does not coincide with reality. They drift further and further into a world of manipulation and control, where fantasy meets a lack of empathy and this collision creates a backwards way of thinking. What would be considered societal norms become confusing concepts to the narcissist who operates solely in the mind, lacking all-natural soulful energy. To successfully be able to apply logic one must possess a connection between mind, body, and soul.

Narcissists have a deep disconnect to their emotions and difficulty regulating themselves. A lack of conscience allows a person to live strictly in their mind, while leaving emotions out of it. The narcissist could never embrace emotions, as they no longer feel them, which causes natural reactions and perception to be skewed.

Narcissistic Personality Disorder is carried by two types of people: psychopaths and sociopaths. Next, we will explore the distinct differences between the calm, cool, and collected psychopath to the highly explosive sociopath.

Chapter 4

Psychopath Versus Sociopath

Psychopath and sociopath are two terms used collectively today, when in fact there is a distinct difference between the two.

Psychopath	Sociopath
Likely to be educated with a good career	Superficial charm
Controlled behavior	Untruthful and manipulative
Highly manipulative	Egocentric
Completely unable to form personal attachments	Devoid of remorse or empathy
Takes calculated risks, participates in fraud schemes; minimizes evidence	Seeks to dominate and win
	Expert storyteller
	Presents themselves heroically with high morals and philosophy
	Incites emotional chaos
	Feigns love to get what they want
	Never apologizes

The psychopath operates in a covert manner; they are calm and charming, skillfully planning each move they make. The sociopath is a loose cannon whose temper runs high and can become extremely aggressive, very quickly. I like to compare these distinct and separate character types to a missile and a hand grenade.

The Missile and the Hand Grenade

Like a guided missile, the psychopath slowly plans an attack, prepares, and strikes when least expected, typically in a covert manner. So, when dealing with this superficial, grandiose personality, it is important to realize that they calculate and control each of their advances of cruelty. The assaults come when least expected, leaving victims confused, disorientated, and shocked.

The sociopath uses a hand grenade to attack. They easily become triggered, pull back, launch, and explode. They tend to be more volatile and temperamental. So, when dealing with a volatile personality, be on guard because the sociopath can be triggered quite easily, and when they go off, there is always an explosion.

A psychopath can carry off the greatest crimes because they can always hold a calm demeanor, especially when confronted with their own lies; without a conscience, they have a complete lack of remorse. There will never be guilt or blame, even when caught red-handed. They will lie to the very end. They fool most people and only do the rare few get to see what lies underneath the mask — and those who see under the mask usually end up dead or psychologically dismantled. The psychopath only experiences pleasure when causing pain and suffering.

According to Scott A. Bonn, PHD, a contributor to *Psychology Today*, there is a clear and distinct difference between a psychopath and sociopath. He claims that sociopaths are jittery, hyper, and prone to emotional outbursts. Because of their volatile nature, they are unable to hold down steady jobs, relationships, or stay in one place too long. The psychopath, however, is unable to develop genuine feeling or form attachments and lacks the ability to experience empathy with others. Psychopaths are highly manipulative and can gain people's trust quite easily.[17]

The important thing to remember is that both the psychopath and sociopath lack a common element: empathy. Neither is capable of genuine feelings of love towards others. They may appear as if they are capable of feelings, care, and understanding by putting on the air of charm and kindness. They may pretend to possess a willingness to help their fellow man but, they will only perform a good deed when they are seeking some sort of recognition, control measure, or payback. Cruel, devious, malicious intentions are the mainstay of both a sociopath and psychopath because they fail to feel remorse for their actions and behavior. Both the sociopath and psychopath are highly dangerous, as they both suffer from anti-personality disorder and violent tendencies.

According to neuroscientist James Fallon, psychopaths are pathological liars, manipulators, and charmers with a detachment from their conscience resulting in a complete lack of empathy/understanding for others and the

[17] Bonn, Scott A. "The Differences Between Psychopaths and Sociopaths." *Psychology Today*, Sussex Publishers, 2018, www.psychologytoday.com/us/blog/wicked-deeds/201801/how-tell-psychopath-sociopath.

[18] Fallon, James. "How I Discovered I Have the Brain of a Psychopath | James Fallon." *The Guardian*, Guardian News and Media, 2 June 2014, www.theguardian.com/commentisfree/2014/jun/03/how-i-discovered-i-have-the-brain-of-a-psychopath.

ability to accept accountability. In constant seeking of stimulation, a psychopath is violent and can be gratified by the pain they inflict in others.

A new area of neuroscience known as "connectomics" seeks to give a kind of unifying theory of the brain. Brain scans are performed to show the difference between "normal" brain patterns and "abnormal" brain patterns (reduced activity in the orbital prefrontal cortex), which indicate psychopathic functioning. Reduced activity in this region plays a role in regulating emotions and impulse control, as well as morality and aggression.

James Fallon, who has made a career studying the mind of criminals, decided to conduct brain scans on his family members, including himself. The results were shocking when they revealed that while his family's brain activity was normal, Mr. Fallon's was abnormal, just as the criminal minds he has studied during his professional career.

"The joke was on me," he says. "It turned out I was the ruffian. I have the exact brain pattern of a psychopathic killer," says Mr. Fallon.[18]

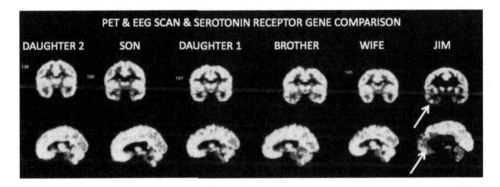

Chapter 5

Tricks of the Trade

The narcissist has an arsenal of tricks up their sleeve used to mentally torture their victims. This chapter will explain their tactics, exposing all they try so desperately to keep hidden underneath the mask.

Love Bombing - How It All Starts

The narcissist is ready to step into the spotlight and get noticed. They have rehearsed this moment many times in their mind, as a much-anticipated adrenaline rush leads them into the gaslighting tango with their unwitting victim. Overwhelming their victim with love, adoration, and praise, the narcissist pulls out all the stops to make sure and create an atmosphere of ease and comfort as victims are blown away by all the things they have in common, from music, art, movies, literature, favorite past times, etc. Remember, the narcissist studies their victims ahead of time to emulate everything from their behavior to likes and dislikes. Every moment is well rehearsed as the narcissist carefully plans each word they say and move they make.

Victims begin to feel at ease as they soak in the euphoria from the illusion of adoration being created. They feel as if they are walking on cloud nine while the narcissist continues to pour on the superficial charm. Smothered with lavish gifts, romantic fantasies and getaways, the unsuspecting victim has no idea what is coming next when the short stay in the "fantasy suite" turns into an extended stay at the "Bates Motel.".

Victims have already become hooked by the strong emotional attachment that has developed and are doomed as the narcissist gears up to knock the victim off the very pedestal, they once placed them on. The victims are now drawn in as a pawn in a game of chess, a game where reality is flipped as the narcissist gains full control of the board. The victim's judgment will be shuffled around so often that they will begin to second guess themselves as the narcissist switches from love and adoration to a devastating devaluation.

Devaluing Stage

That feeling of bonding and love the victim thought was being reciprocated by the narcissist was all just a big illusion. Reality sets in, as if almost overnight the narcissist becomes bitterly cold and unfeeling. The personality and overall attitude they seemed to enjoy has now become a point of contention as the narcissist slowly tries to create the illusion that they are the victim of the one they are about to abuse. The narcissist rolled with the punches up until now, keeping a score sheet the whole time of all the victim's wrong doings, which the narcissist will use an excuse to abuse. The narcissist starts to make the victim feel as if the behavior they are about to receive is warranted because they made the narcissist angry; they deserve it. All the victim's flaws and the new ones the narcissist is looking to lie about are used to paint the victim in the worst light possible in order to gain sympathy from others as they move undetected behind the scenes, pretending to be the victim of an undesirable person who perhaps needs constant supervision.

Victims now become drawn into an emotionally abusive vortex where every conversation, every interaction, flows in a nonsensical, circular motion. The "nice" narcissist has now become bitterly cold and unfeeling, which leaves victims in a state of confusion. They cannot understand what just happened. The narcissist was agreeable, lovable, kind, and fun to be with; now they are looking in the eyes of a stranger, desperately trying to find the person they thought they fell in love with. The victim is left feeling emotionally battered and confused. There is no resolution to the issue, no sense of compromise or a win/win outcome. It feels like the narcissist needs to win regardless of the issue or what is at stake. The victim is left feeling unsupported and misunderstood.

Every single detail shared with the narcissist now becomes what they use to exploit their victim, as well as falsehoods fabricated by the narcissist as they humiliate, belittle, and degrade. Their goal is to break and destroy the spirit the victim until they become an empty shell of the person they once were.

They want victims to succumb to their every opinion and point of view, agree with everything they say, and when victims do not fall in line, they become a targeted enemy almost in an instant. All the times the victim, disagreed with the narcissist become the fuel behind a level of hate, anger and distain, like a freight train in motion that cannot be stopped and only continues to pick up speed as the victim hangs on for dear life, screaming "get me off this ride."

Projection

A narcissist will set up the illusion that any good deed you have done, they have done and every bad deed they have done, you've done. They like to project all their bad qualities on to others while trying to assume possession of the good qualities of others. They feel that playing this little game lets them remain shame- and guilt-free, which allows them to continue their cruelty.

A narcissist can be caught red-handed, and they will deny the event ever took place. They would rather their victims assume accountability for their actions. Just like the example above, we can now see that a narcissist operates in reverse. The strong presence of an anti-social personality causes them to behave in an illusion of their fostered reality. Logic does not prevail, as the narcissist will always appear "different" from others. The narcissist refuses to accept imperfection and casts their flaws onto others. They use the victim's flaws as a tool to exploit, while promoting themselves as a good, well-balanced person.

Narcissists always escape accountability in every aspect of their life. They live this fantasy, guilt -free life with no regrets because they make sure the world carries these things for them. A narcissist cannot bear shame; they project this onto others.

A narcissist can be quite revealing during every attempt at projection because they reveal themselves with all the untrue things they say of others. If a narcissist is accusing their victim of doing something they are not doing, it is almost a guarantee that is exactly what the narcissist is really doing; so, in essence, they just gave themselves away by the hateful lies they try and get others to believe of the victim and the victim to believe of themselves. Some victims start believing the horrible things being said about them and begin slipping into a self-fulfilling prophecy.

A self-fulfilling prophecy occurs when a person is constantly bullied into believing they are a worthless human being. The victim will embrace the horrible way they are being treated as if they deserve it.

Gaslighting

Gaslighting is a consistent pattern of malicious behavior designed to provoke emotional responses, which over time destroy the mainframe of a person's mental equilibrium. Those responses become heightened and are used to portray the victim as crazy, unstable, and the aggressor, when they are only responding to how they are being treated.

When someone consistently accuses the victim of doing/saying something they did not do or say, it causes extreme distress and provokes emotionally charged reactions. Thrown off balance from each well-planned, cruel attack, the victim shakes and trembles, gripped with fear and anxiety at what the narcissist will do next. Gaslighting is insidious and eats away at the very core of a person's whole being.

Reid interrogation method

Law officials commonly use the Reid Interrogation method when trying to pull confessions from those they believe guilty. However, this method is too often used on innocent people, which can result in false confessions.

In a study conducted with college students, Julia Shaw and her fellow researchers in forensic psychology were able to show just how easily individuals can be manipulated. After three hours of being given misinformation and encouragement, 70 percent of students believed they had committed a crime and some even remembered specific details of a crime that never took place.[19]

People think it cannot happen to them when in fact it can happen to anyone. Even those who have never committed a criminal act in their life can become convinced they performed a criminal act. So how did they create false memories in the minds of those never in contact with the police?

Elizabeth Loftus, a cognitive psychologist at University of California states that it is somewhat like a page online that others can edit, but not you. Once someone is convinced something is true, their imagination mixes with their past experiences and become so intertwined and internalized that "truth and fiction become one."

If these kinds of "false confessions" can be achieved in a controlled study, just imagine when this method is used by a narcissist as part of the gaslighting process inside an intimate environment. Victims of psychological abuse are made to endure countless exhausting hours listening to stories of being in places, with people, and doing things they have not done. Narcissists

---

[19] Siegel, Nathan. "You Can Be Persuaded to Confess to An Invented Crime, Study Finds." NPR, 30 Jan. 2015, www.npr.org/2015/01/29/382483367/you-can-be-convinced-to-confess-to-an-invented-crime-study-finds.

will repeat this technique day after day. Sometimes a victim will refuse to give in to the narcissist's "delusional thoughts" and stand their ground, refusing to admit to something they did not do. This leads to the victim experiencing emotional exhaustion, throwing off the mental equilibrium and state of being. The victim, while in a state of complete unrest, will still stand in the truth, refusing to give in. When the narcissist has presented a story, with no proof that was never admitted to, they will move on and just when the victim feels that moment of soulful rest they so desperately need, the narcissist will zero in with another round of intense, torturous interrogation, as it's time to break down the victim again.

Different scenarios are presented to the victim after the one before has been worn down with no confession. This type of abuse is pure terror, as the narcissist is using the exact tactics law officials use in their interrogation room.

Interrogations are justified by making the victim feel they are responsible for the narcissist's mistrust. Victims maintain highly defensive posture when exposed to repeated rounds of abuse, becoming emotionally unbalanced and eruptive. This is the perfect tool for the cunning narcissist to keep their victim completely off balance. The victims never have a chance to gain any posture because the narcissist is ready to tear them back down again through another round of emotional/mental torture.

Make no mistake about it: nobody has the right to do this to anyone. Some people will break down and admit to lies just to get the interrogation session over with, whereas other victims stand their ground and remain defiant, which breaks down their whole being (mind, sprit, body) over time. The fact that victims make it out alive and can stand strong is a pure testament to the human spirit.

Narcissists use this type of abuse because it accomplishes a few things. First, it allows the narcissist to cast all their wrong doings on their victim by accusing them of being a horrible, sleazy, low-life person who sleeps with everyone, which is what the narcissist is doing. It also allows for the excuse of "mistrust" that the victim deserves. For example, maybe they draw too much attention while out because they are attractive. The narcissist will blame the victim for the unwanted attention by blaming it on their beauty, not the people who have no right to disrespect the victim.

Withholding

Withholding involves holding back praise, acknowledgment, and agreement, or even cutting off all communication. It is typically used to gain some measure of control over the victim. It keeps the victim in the dark for the most part and has a heavy impact on their emotional state of mind.

Withholding is also used as a bullying tactic to control, manipulate, and cause confusion with the concealment of information, leaving the victim to fill in the blanks. The narcissist takes "remaining a mystery" to a whole new level by purposely not sharing what they think, say, or do, which causes enormous frustration, triggering the most explosive outbursts from their victim. The more emotional the victim becomes, the more satisfied the narcissist.

Narcissists withhold sex, causing the victim to feel insecure and start questioning themselves. This makes the narcissist more desirable as the victim tries harder to gain back the attention that has suddenly been taken away. The victim does everything imaginable to try and make themselves noticed, which the narcissist equates to groveling. This groveling provides the narcissist the perfect supply, as they view this behavior as demeaning, which delights and disgusts the narcissist all at the same time. Most narcissists who are withholding will stay out later and come home smelling of perfume to further up their game. This causes the victim to experience extreme loss of confidence, thinking that the narcissist is out having sex with others and does not care if it is known it or not.

The Silent Treatment

Covert narcissists employ the silent treatment after the victim is left stunned and disorientated from a round of abuse. This is the perfect time for the narcissist to throw more fuel on the fire, knowing the victim will scramble to try and find answers for the cruel behavior that just took place. Victims often beg and plead as emotions skyrocket, but the narcissist will remain calm, stoic even, typically staring straight ahead while the victim tries relentlessly to find answers. This serves to further disorientate the victim, leaving them to fill in the blanks, while believing they are somehow responsible for the horrible treatment. The narcissist wants their victim to believe that every form of bad treatment coming will be their fault and should be held 100 percent accountable, while the narcissist remains blame free. The emotional reaction of the victim creates the illusion that the victim is the aggressor.

By this point, the victim has already been broken down, and the devious narcissist wants to create the ultimate environment of discomfort. Victims feel uneasy and fearful, as if they are walking on eggshells. During this abusive tactic, victims feel as if they are suffocating when in the presence of the narcissist.

Triangulation

The narcissist uses triangulation to create an illusion of desirability. This draws victims into the drama and chaos the narcissist carefully planned.

According to Bree Bonchay LCSW, a specialist in the field of narcissistic abuse, triangulation is divided into four categories:[20]

1. Killing two birds with one stone: The narcissist forever craves control over others and will set up an illusion that they are desired and wanted by someone else to stir up feelings of jealousy, which sparks a rivalry. This provides supply to the crafty narcissist, as well as the control they are looking for. In a healthy relationship people do not invoke feelings of jealousy or insecurity.
2. Recruiting reinforcements: Narcissists use people as tools to settle differences to make what they are saying acceptable and credible by using persuasion, embarrassment, or guilt.
3. Splitting: Splitting pits two people against each other while the narcissist smears the character of one or both individuals, which allows the narcissist to maintain their false image. If their victim is growing tired or aware of the manipulation, the narcissist will pique their interest back up by displaying the great interaction they are having with someone else. For this to work, the narcissist must make sure these two parties are unable to share information or is ready to put a different spin on things. Narcissists love strife, drama, and chaos, and this is a perfect way for them to create it.
4. The pre-discard and dump: When the narcissist is ready to discard the current victim, they will confide in others long before this happens to give the narcissist a credible platform to stand on, while making the victim appear as the abuser to outsiders. Since the narcissist won't allow someone to break ties, they are the ones with the final say. When they exit the victim's life, they do it swiftly and cut off all

---

[20] Bonchay, Bree. "The 4 Most Common Narc-Sadistic Triangulation Tactics." *Free from Toxic*, 25 Feb. 2018, www.freefromtoxic.com/2015/05/13/the-4-most-common-narc-sadistic-triangulation-tactics/.

contact, even when contact is necessary, such as sharing children. Narcissists love to go silent.

Abuse by Proxy

The angry narcissist is ready for a vendetta after finally discarding the victim for good. The victim no longer serves as a source of supply, and now the narcissist has moved on to a new prey. The goal this time is to use the new supply against the old supply. The narcissist is angry and wants revenge, therefore will devise a new plan, sit quietly while the new supply and others the narcissist has gathered up begin to attack the victim. The narcissist will encourage these attacks while creating the illusion they have been wounded by the "crazy, unstable" victim, so others begin backing them up as they become justified in their actions. When a narcissist fears being exposed, they will work extra hard to portray the victim as a liar, a storyteller, effectively ruining the victim's credibility when speaking of the abuse.

People who sing the praises of the narcissists and buy into everything they say are typically outside the narcissist's community because the narcissist would prefer people stay far away, as they are easily manipulated and fooled. The narcissist orchestrates illusions in anticipation of the victim's responses to the bullying by these engaged outsiders. The narcissist would never receive praise of any kind within their own community. They will claim they receive praise, however, like everything else, it is simply a lie.

The Goal of a Smear Campaign

The narcissist starts planting seeds of doubt in the minds of others by exploiting the victim's flaws to justify their abusive tactics and paint themselves a caring, devoted victim themselves. Stories become twisted as blatant lies or half-truths start circulating and the victim starts receiving distain from others, not understanding why.

These vendettas are a result of broken ties; typically the narcissist has discarded the victim during this stage, as the victim no longer serves a purpose, or perhaps the victim has caused extreme narcissistic injury. Either way, now they are out for blood as they devise the perfect plan for revenge. It could take months or it could take years; it makes no difference to the narcissist because once they formulate a plan of attack it can be long and drawn out with many moves along the way. Calculated and methodical, they continue to maneuver the chessboard long after the victim has turned into a ghost. They continue to play, pretending the victim is not there, but they really are. The victim now becomes the scapegoat, and the one responsible for it all. If it were not for victim, their life would be so different, so much better.

The victim's reputation is stomped on; the narcissist is busy behind the scenes changing the way people think of the victim and the narcissist themselves. They want sympathy from wherever they can get it to show that others agree with their distorted viewpoints and back up the way the narcissist feels about their victim. The narcissist will continue until the victim's reputation has been annihilated. Many victims suffer great losses during this time, such as financial, family, etc. Support systems slowly begin to crumble, destroying their very foundation, which inevitably leaves them feeling isolated and alone.

Baiting and Bashing

The favorite framing game of an abusive personality is baiting and bashing. Narcissists use this method to make their victim do things that portray them as the abuser. A narcissist will set the victim up to fail and exploit them for it, as well use any past indiscretions, emotional reactions, and flaws to paint them as the abuser. Narcissists degrade, dehumanize, demoralize, devalue, and disgrace their victims to get people on "their side" of a war they have now waged against the unsuspecting victim.

This effectively shifts any focus of them onto the victim in the minds of those the narcissist is trying to convince. A narcissist will do this as a bullying tactic to further break down an already suffering victim. Victims typically try and defend lies being spread around about them and come across as crazy, which further backs up the narcissist's false claims. Remaining guilt-free, as others do their bullying for them, the narcissist is delighted with the external supply they receive from the previous victim's reactions. This sparks the flames that keep burning the discarded victim long after the abuse should have ended.

During this time, the narcissist thrives while the victim loses all their support and becomes isolated, paranoid, worried, scared, and empty inside. This prevents the victim from healing and only adds more abuse. The victim is still caught in the cycle of abuse, even though the narcissist makes it look like they have nothing to do with it and professes to others how they want nothing to do with the discarded victim. Because of this, each time the victim reacts to being gaslit, the narcissist uses the reaction to convince others the victim is chasing after them and wants them back. Typically victims try so hard to bring peace when this happens. They just want the abuse to stop, so they will often approach the narcissist to apologize because deep down inside they have been programmed to feel they are responsible for the anger they receive from the narcissist.

Narcissists are so good at mind games; it is no wonder they are brilliant at playing the victim.

Parent Alienation

Parent alienation is when a child develops contempt and hate toward the victimized parent and begins to reject them for unwarranted reasons. Children in this position often view the alienating parent as the "good parent" and have total distain for the victimized parent. Contact minimizes as the child rejects and refuses communication at the encouragement or demands of the alienating parent.

So, attached to the alienating parent, the child will never realize that they are being taught to hate; they are too innocent to understand what brainwashing is. Children also do not say anything because they feel if they do, the alienating parent will not love them anymore. The more the child agrees with the narcissist, the more praise and reward they receive; children consider it good behavior when they go along with the feelings of the alienating parent and truly start to believe their nurturing parent is a horrible person they should stay away from.

There is never any co-parenting to be had with a narcissist who has gained control over their children. Their goal is to have the other parent eliminated, by whatever means possible. Children become the weapon of choice for the narcissist as they instill the same hate and rage in the minds of their children they possess towards the victimized parent.

Narcissists do not genuinely care for their children and are more concerned with how they can use and manipulate the children to tear apart all bonds with the victimized parent and display them a prize they won over the other parent. In their game of revenge, children become the perfect weapons in the narcissist's arsenal.

No child should be considered a traitor simply for loving the other parent.

Narcissists view their children as trophies to be displayed as a measure of their own personal achievement. They are a by-product of how great and wonderful the narcissist portrays themselves to be. The rest of world needs to revere them as the incredible parent that they give the illusion they are when what is really happening never seems to leave the narcissist's clan.

Now the narcissist is ready to put their plan of action in place as praise turns to threats, degrading comments, shifting blame, criticizing manipulating, verbally assaulting, dominating, blackmailing, withdrawing, and withholding love and affection. The narcissist is preparing to throw gas on the newly ignited flames of psychological terror that have only just begun, as the victim enters the dark realm of abuse. The intimate connection established in the beginning of the relationship is now what will keep the victim locked in the cycle of abuse, otherwise known as "trauma bonding."

Chapter 6

Stockholm Syndrome/Trauma Bonding

Stockholm syndrome got its name from a bank robbery that took place in Stockholm, Sweden on August 23, 1973 when two men carrying machine guns held three women hostage for several days. By the time this was over, the women had become attached to their captors. One woman took their side by defending them to the media and police. Another one of the women even became engaged to one of the robbers while another woman spent quite a sum of money for one robber's lawyer.[21]

According to Kathryn Wescott, editor for BBC News, the term was most recently applied an Australian case involving Natascha Kampusch. Wolfgang Priklopil kidnapped Kampusch at age 10 and locked her in a cellar for 10 years. When her captor died, she cried and lit a candle as he lay in the mortuary.[22] Stockholm syndrome creates extreme trauma and this becomes the bond that ties victims to their abusers.

Trauma bonding occurs in abusive interpersonal relations and is often recognized by an obvious imbalance of power. A high intensity, unstable environment can shift quickly from periods of kindness to extended periods of cruelty; when the two mix, the trauma the victim experiences bonds them to their abuser. These bonds can last long after the relationship ties have been severed.

Donald G. Dutton, from the Department of Psychology at the University of British Columbia, and Susan Painter from the Department of Psychology at the Carleton University claim strong emotional attachments develop from two features within an abusive relationship and they are an imbalance of power and intermittent good to bad treatment.[23]

Joseph M. Carver, Ph.D., clinical psychologist, states Stockholm syndrome (SS) can be found in any type of interpersonal relationship. In these

[21] Lambert, Laura. "Stockholm Syndrome." *Encyclopædia Britannica*, Encyclopædia Britannica, Inc., 27 Apr. 2018, www.britannica.com/science/Stockholm-syndrome.
[22] Westcott, Kathryn. "Hope for the Children of the Cellar." BBC News, 28 Apr. 2008, news.bbc.co.uk/2/hi/europe/7370889.stm.
[23] Descilo, Teresa. "UNDERSTANDING AND TREATING TRAUMATIC BONDS." Trauma Therapy Articles, 2009, www.healing-arts.org/healing_trauma_therapy/traumabonding-traumaticbonds.htm.

situations, the abuser is in a "position of control or authority."[24] Once Stockholm syndrome is understood, it becomes easier to empathize with victims and the rationale that causes them to stay with their abusive partner. Dr. Carver realizes that "every syndrome has symptoms or behaviors and Stockholm syndrome is no exception."[25] Although there is nothing etched in stone about Stockholm syndrome in romantic relationships, Dr. Carver, has frequently found these features present in victims:

- Positive feelings toward their abuser
- The development of negative feelings by the victim toward those closest to them (family members, friends, etc.)
- Avoidance of any belief that they are in trouble and need to be rescued
- 100 percent supportive of the abuser
- Assisting the abuser, even if that means going against their moral code
- Cutting off all those trying to help[26]

Narcissists love corrupting their victims into becoming manipulative and deceptive — just like they are. The goal for a narcissist is to destroy their victims from the inside out and pierce straight to the moral core of their being. They pursue, capture, isolate, corrupt, dominate, and finally discard victims, one at a time, each serving their own unique purpose.

Stockholm syndrome has been cited numerous times in kidnapping and hostage cases, most typically those involving women. For example, when revolutionary militants kidnapped Patty Hearst, a Californian newspaper heiress, in 1974, she developed sympathy for her captors and joined them in their robbery, which resulted in a prison sentence. However, her lawyer argued she had been brainwashed and was suffering from Stockholm syndrome, which gave her irrational feelings toward her captors she otherwise would not be experiencing.[27]

Narcissists like to keep their victims in line by creating a trauma bond, which keeps them captive. No matter the circumstances, this bond tears down the unwitting victim's emotional well-being and mental equilibrium. It can leave

---

[24] Carver, Joseph M. "The "Small Kindness" Perception." *Love and Stockholm Syndrome*, 2016, drjoecarver.makeswebsites.com/clients/49355/File/love_and_stockholm_syndrome.html.
[25] Carver, 2016.
[26] Carver, 2016.
[27] "Patty Hearst." FBI, 18 May 2016, www.fbi.gov/history/famous-cases/patty-hearst.

a devastating imprint. Even though this a place of horror for most, it is can also be a place of comfort for victims.

Inside the abusive relationship, the narcissist switches between many Dr. Jekyll and Mr. Hyde presentations: turning from warm too cold within seconds, causing the victim to believe they are responsible for the sudden change in mood.

Victims stay in this cycle of abuse, as the bad times outweigh the good times; the victim is given positive reinforcement only to be broken down again. This push-pull environment creates a unique level of confusion, during which victims run to the narcissist for validation, clarification, and approval that they are behaving as the narcissist wishes. This is what keeps them bonded as they become totally dependent on the narcissist to validate their own existence. The victim has been reduced to a mere version of the former self who is now exclusively dependent on approval and overly sensitive to disapproval.

It's so hard for victims to believe the mental games the narcissist uses can occur from someone they feel so bonded with; any normal person does not behave this way. Victims cannot deny their feeling of what they believe to be love, a feeling that the narcissist uses to control and manipulate but doesn't reciprocate. Even when victims break free, the bond remains long after relationship ties have been severed.

It's hard to get to the healing process when there is no clear understanding of what's happening — that's where family and friends of victims come in. Providing support and understanding is key when trying to bring the victim back to reality. After all, their reality has been transformed and is skewed; they desperately need to see the truth. The truth can be a hard pill to swallow, which is why victims have a hard time accepting the vicious cycle they are caught up in. It's like being addicted to a drug: there is nothing to subdue the pain of withdrawal as victims suffer in silent agony and crave that intimate bond, no matter how bad it might have been. So, the more people in their support circle that recognize the effort it takes for the victim break away from the narcissist, the better.

Nobody should be subjected to such horrid treatment, but narcissists are effective at making victims believe they deserve what they get; the narcissist has made them feel fortunate to have them in their lives, when this is the furthest thing from the truth. Feelings of worthlessness set in after time, and most victims find themselves isolated, scared, shamed, and all alone. They need people to be there for them, no matter how hard they make it. If friends or family members maintain a certain posture, it will only make things worse for the already suffering victim. For example, telling a victim, "I am trying to help, but you stay. You're digging your own grave, I'm out of here" only further isolates the individual. The victim will sink them further into the hole they are instinctually trying to climb out of.

Once a victim starts getting clarity, they can begin to move away from their abuser. This book is geared to providing just that kind of clarity, for both victims/survivors and friends and family members alike.

Now we have looked at the tactics used to abuse and the trauma bonding that takes place once the victim has become "blinded by love," let us delve into the heart of the matter. We will peak underneath the mask as the narcissist throws gas on a fire already burning, with seething anticipation that leads the victim into a dance through the scorching flames of the gaslighting effect.

Chapter 7

The Gaslighting Effect

Gaslighting is a form of psychological abuse in which the abuser consistently accuses the victim of saying or doing something they did not say or do, which causes extreme distress to the victim. They second-guess their own memory, perception, and judgment. Those who use the gaslighting technique want to rewrite their victim's reality so that they adopt the new reality being fed to them as their own. The gaslighting effect, commonly used by dictators, is successful when a lie, presented often enough, becomes embraced as the truth.

According to Darlene Lancer, JD, LMFT of Psychology Today: "Gaslighting is a malicious and hidden form of mental and emotional abuse, designed to plant seeds of self-doubt and alter one's perception of reality." [28]

Anyone can fall victim to gaslighting, from any walk of life, and it can happen in a variety of interpersonal relations, including with friends, family, colleagues, and romantic partners. The very nature of gaslighting is such that one can never fully understand it unless they have experienced it, and even then, it is hard to believe.

Gaslighting involves a pattern of malicious behavior designed to provoke emotional responses and destroy the mainframe of a person's mental equilibrium. Those responses become heightened and are then used to portray the victim as unstable, crazy, and an abuser. The victim begins to believe they are the problem and assume blame for the abuser's anger, thinking they must have done something wrong to deserve this to rationalize their aggressive, cruel behavior. Nobody could imagine someone intentionally hurting them for no reason, so they believe they must be the reason. Normal people do not have the ability to see this kind of abuse. It is not within the realm of rationale, so they do not understand or realize what exactly is happening to them and even have a hard time describing it. Victims simply know something is very wrong.

Narcissists thrive off reactions, so they intentionally create all the scenarios imaginable to provoke the most emotionally charged responses.

---

[28] Lancer, Darlene. "How to Know If You're a Victim of Gaslighting." *Psychology Today*, Sussex Publishers, 2018, www.psychologytoday.com/ca/blog/toxic-relationships/201801/how-know-if-youre-victim-gaslighting.

The term "gaslighting" is based on the 1938 play written by Patrick Hamilton that made the silver screen in 1944 in George Cukor's Movie "Gaslight". Ingrid Bergman played a young, sweet girl named Paula who witnessed the murder of her aunt in their family home. Years later, Paula would go on to marry a narcissist Gregory (Charles Boyer) and return to the family home where her aunt was murdered.[29]

Over time, Paula begins to doubt her own sanity as her husband tries to convince her she is becoming forgetful and too emotionally explosive, that she is going mentally insane. He purposely does things like move pictures, dim lights, and bang on the walls to make her believe she is losing her mind and imagining it all. [30]

Since the term comes from a movie, its definition is specific: when lies are repeated with confidence, the victim begins to doubt their own sanity and believe the lies to be truth. In this move, Stockholm Syndrome develops as well; the victim is uncertain they can perceive reality correctly, and they look to the narcissistic gaslighter for clarification, creating a strong trauma bond of attachment.[31]

Narcissists using the gaslighting technique act hurt and indignant. They play the victim when challenged or questioned. Covert manipulation easily turns into overt abuse with accusations targeted at the victim that claim they are distrustful, ungrateful, disrespectful, unkind, overly sensitive, too emotional, dishonest, stupid, insecure, emotionally damaged, worthless, and so on. Abuse may escalate to anger and intimidation followed by punishment, threats, or bullying if the author doesn't embrace the false reality, they are trying to feed the victim.

The consistent lies and falsehoods presented by the narcissist have the potential to be embraced by the victim as the truth, which is known as the illusory truth effect and is at the base of all gaslighting activity.

Gaslighting is an illusory truth, known as the illusory-truth effect, which was first observed by Hasher, Goldstein, and Toppino (1977). They found that subjects rated repeated statements as more probably true than new statements. Repetition is an illogical basis for truth; Wittgenstein likened the tendency to believe repeated information to buying a second newspaper to see if the first one was right. Although repetition does not provide evidence for truth,

[29] Wilkinson, Alissa. "What Is Gaslighting? The 1944 Film Gaslight Is the Best Explainer." Vox, 21 Jan. 2017, www.vox.com/culture/2017/1/21/14315372/what-is-gaslighting-gaslight-movie-ingrid-bergman.

[30] Wilkinson, 2017.

[31] Wilkinson, 2017.

repetition does increase familiarity. Therefore, when a lie is presented with consistency, victims may begin to embrace it as truth, which is why the illusory truth is so effective. [32]

The abuser wants their victim's self-worth to plummet by hoping they assume feelings of worthlessness through their barrage of verbal assaults, subtle innuendos, and twisted mind games. Some victims assume a self-fulfilling prophecy when they start to feel just as the abuser is painting them to be. Once they begin to think and imagine a host of bad things about themselves, their sense of self begins to slip away.

Since the whole basis of gaslighting is projection — a lie becomes truth, and truth becomes a lie — and the narcissist is forever accusing their victims of doing things they are really doing such as cheating, lying, and playing games, etc., this common manipulation tactic is known as the pre-emptive strike. According to Stephanie A. Sarkis, Ph.D. of *Psychology Today*, the narcissist shifts all the blame onto the victim, which takes the spotlight off of what they are really doing.[33]

This manipulative tactic is so effective because when the victim is accused of what the gaslighter is really doing, the victim is now put in a spot where they have to prove something that never happened. This escalates to an emotional imbalance in the victim, who is busy trying to defend something that never took place, giving them little to no time to focus on the narcissist's gaslighting behavior. [34]

According to Sarkis, "Gaslighters, people who try to control others through manipulation, will often accuse others of behaviors that they are engaged in themselves. This is a classic manipulation tactic." [35]

The narcissist may even make it look like the victim is doing them wrong by providing fake evidence to back up their claim. They will also omit facts when describing an event to make it look different from how it really took place. People that are being fed these falsehoods by the crafty narcissist will buy into the drama and stay hooked by the narcissist's endless supply of juicy, prefabricated events and conversations that never really took place.[36]

---

[32] Begg, Ian Maynard. "Dissociation of Processes of Belief; Source Recollection, Statement Familiarity, and the Illusion of Truth." 1992, citeseerx.ist.psu.edu.
[33] Sarkis, Stephanie A. "Why Gaslighters Accuse You of Gaslighting." *Psychology Today*, Sussex Publishers, 2017, www.psychologytoday.com/ca/blog/here-there-and-everywhere/201702/why-gaslighters-accuse-you-gaslighting.
[34] Sarkis, 2017.
[35] Sarkis, 2017.
[36] Sarkis, 2017.

The goal of gaslighting is to target the victim's self-worth, self-confidence, and emotional state of being so they no longer function independently but become more and more dependent on their abuser to validate their own existence. Gaslighting. when performed effectively over time, may cause victims to slip into submission and feelings of worthlessness.

Gaslighting can be performed in a variety of different ways.

Because narcissists love strife and chaos they will do anything to start a problem. They do this with an intention to keep it going for as long as possible, which breaks down and emotionally weakens the victim. To justify their contemptuous malicious attacks, they will claim the victim started the problem.

Innuendoes like "silly, you must have forgotten," or "no, you didn't tell me that," and "you told me last night, don't you remember" often lead some victims to believe they are suffering from dementia or drifting into Alzheimer's, as their memory is the target in their gaslighting experience.

Some narcissists do not care if they flaunt that they are with other women, so the victim spins out of control emotionally while they laugh and continue to dangle their indiscretions, all while painting an unflattering image of their victim. Confronting them about it gives the narcissist the emotional response they seek, so they will keep it going while they offer the victim no freedom to escape the abuse. The narcissist actively denies any wrongdoing while making sure the victim believes it's all in their head.

The Reid interrogation method is a gaslighting tactic used to create an illusion and/or story that is presented to the victim as fact. This could even be a detailed account of something the narcissist did themselves; it is a falsehood they want their victim to own up to. Victims will endure hours of heavy questions and statements such as, "Why did you do that?" or "Why are you denying it; we both know it happened." When questions like this are repeated, the effects are deadly. The victim's defenses are so high, they shake inside with fear right to the very core of their being.

A narcissist takes great pleasure in gaslighting their victim in public with grandiose displays of humiliation — overly flirtatious with serving staff, staring inappropriately at the opposite sex, saying something to upset the victim, centering the victim out inappropriately — that is designed to provoke emotional outbursts that backs up the narcissist's claim of mental instability to onlookers. Victims are met with the silent treatment as the atmosphere is cold as ice, all of which has been carefully pre-planned by the narcissist.

The narcissist may also elect to attack the victim's spiritual core with such comments as, "I am God; you don't need HIM" and/or "you need to get right with God." This causes the victim to question their faith; if that is not bad enough, it leaves them with a feeling they are not acceptable in the eyes of God. They want to attack a person's core by eliminating their soul, spirit, and faith. So, if God does not love them, they must be truly worthless, just like the narcissist is trying to portray. Turning the victim against their place of worship would be the ultimate accomplishment because the gaslighter inevitably wants the victim to worship them. Narcissists do not believe in God because they are too busy believing they are a god.

Stephanie A. Sarkis Ph.D. of *Psychology Today*, claims people who gaslight typically uses the following techniques:

Telling blatant lies
They say an obvious, flat-out lie with a straight face to set a precedent after telling a huge lie. Victims will not know if they are ever being told the truth, which keeps them off-kilter.

Deny, even though there's proof
A narcissist could be caught red-handed, and they will still have some way of explaining it away. There could be mounting proof to show them, and they will still deny they did anything wrong.

Destroy the foundation
They use those closest to the victim as ammunition, including their children and their family. They know how important kids and family are to victims, so they may be one of the first things they attack. If the victim has kids, the gaslighter will tell the victim that they should not have had the children.

Victim shaming
Narcissists will claim their victim to be a unworthy person by listing a long list of negative traits so others will empathize with the narcissist who is dealing with a "crazy person".

They break down their victim over time
This is one of the insidious things about gaslighting: it is done gradually with a lie here and there, a snide comment every so often, and then it starts ramping up. Even the brightest, most self-aware people can be sucked into gaslighting — it is that effective.

The narcissist's actions never match their words
In this case, actions speak louder than words. What they say means nothing — it is what they are doing that is the issue.

Positive reinforcement that is designed to fool the victim

The narcissist that cuts down the victim also builds them up. The person who just said the victim had no value suddenly speaks of their value. Typically, the value is of the victim did something to serve the narcissist's best interests.[37]

It starts with subtle mind game such as making plans and claiming the victim did not hear right or claiming the victim is lying to them. It is a slow, insidious process that leaves the victim totally confused and perplexed, wondering what just happened. Facts become distorted and victims begin to question their reality, judgment, and state of mind; they turn to the narcissist for clarification and ask why they are being treated so badly. Most victims believe their abuser will get better — just give it time and they will be nice again. But sadly, nice never happens once the "cruel switch" has been turned on. Any niceties will be strictly an act to get the victim feeling good again before the next attack.

By this point, the narcissist has studied their victim long enough to know how to effectively push buttons and achieve the desired responses. The gaslighting effect kicks into full swing when they are criticized, and where there appeared to be sympathy has suddenly changed to distain and antagonism. At this point, the victim's feelings are met with silence, or everything they say is minimized or twisted, causing even more confusion.

Narcissists thrive off strife, chaos, and drama and will do anything to keep it going for as long as possible. The whole experience causes the victim to break down, as they are emotionally weakened. To justify their contemptuous, malicious behavior, the narcissist will project their actions on to the victim, simply stating phrases like "you started it" or "it's because of you". Once the victim has a chance to relax, the narcissist will emotionally charge them again. The cycle gets more intense over time and breaks down all the victim's natural defenses.

---

[37] Sarkis, Stephanie A. "11 Warning Signs of Gaslighting." *Psychology Today,* Sussex Publishers, 2017, www.psychologytoday.com/us/blog/here-there-and-everywhere/201701/11-warning-signs-gaslighting.

At this point, the narcissist starts to gauge weaknesses, which in their mind are sensitiveness and natural human emotions. These sensitivities will be used to agitate the victim into planned and controlled reactions.

The narcissist carefully continues to manipulate the victim's sense of reality as it slowly becomes distorted, allowing the narcissist the opportunity to say, "it's all in your head" or "you're too sensitive." The narcissist has zero tolerance for their personal boundaries and will step right over them to get what they want. In the narcissist's mind, their victim is not allowed to have thoughts and opinions of their own. Victims eventually begin to question everything they do and say in fear of the retaliation from the narcissist and have a hard time discerning fact from fiction.

Shahida Arabi, bestselling author and graduate of Columbia University, claims narcissists intertwine lies with partial truths to make victims feelings seem ridiculous, when all they were trying to do is express their feelings. Doing this, she says, "enables them to invalidate your right to have thoughts and emotions about their inappropriate behavior and instills in you a sense of guilt when you attempt to establish boundaries."[38]

Initially, victims react to the overwhelming gaslighting with disbelief and shock and cannot understand what is happening to them. They know something is terribly wrong, that they are not being treated normally, but they have trouble understanding what is happening, which is precisely what the gaslighter wants. If their victim knew what was being done to them, it would not work. Therefore this type of abuse is so effective at disorientating the unwitting victim.

Narcissists will also use their victim's flaws and embellish the truth in efforts to exploit them as less than a perfect in their court of public opinion. The abuser will then use that to portray themselves the hero, saving the victim from themselves. This allows them to justify their abusive tactics to outsiders. The narcissist is gaslighting their victim and outsiders alike into believing the victim will deserve the psychological terror the awaits.

The narcissist will be especially careful not to let their mask tilt while making sure all the victim's family, friends, and co-workers like them. They will later use that same support system to bring the victim down by planting seeds of doubt in the minds of those closest to the victim. The goal is to establish

---

[38] Arabi, Shahida. "20 Diversion Tactics Highly Manipulative Narcissists, Sociopaths and Psychopaths Use to Silence You." Thought Catalog, 5 Oct. 2018, thoughtcatalog.com/shahida-arabi/2016/06/20-diversion-tactics-highly-manipulative-narcissists-sociopaths-and-psychopaths-use-to-silence-you/10/.

control over each person, so they can be removed one by one, eventually leaving the victim standing alone.

Now the narcissist will begin pulling the puppet strings and start maneuvering the world around their victim in unimaginable ways. Covertly, they are actively chipping away at the very infrastructure of the victim. They annihilate every support system by planting seed of doubt, not only the victim's mind but also everyone the victim believes they can trust. Friends, family, and acquaintances start behaving differently toward the victim for no apparent reason, which further disorientates and confuses the victim. The victim has a hard time processing why people seem to be turning against them for no reason. Victims either start cutting people off at the encouragement of the narcissist or outsiders start believing all the lies spread by the narcissist behind the victim's back and either way, the narcissist is succeeding at eliminating and isolating the victim.

Victims become so uncomfortable that they retreat from their loved ones and withdraw, becoming isolated. While victims retreat, the narcissist uses these public displays to increase their value with members of the opposite sex and typically have a night out with someone else. Here is when they can gain sympathy from others, claiming to be the victim of a mentally ill partner who belongs at home.

The more agitated their victim gets, the more satisfied the narcissist becomes. This causes extreme stress and confusion and the fleeting moments of joy are now becoming a distant memory as the victim starts experiencing a full-on attack, with no understanding as to why. Isolated and alone with only the narcissist to speak with, the narcissist is now ready to drive them over the edge.

Unable to trust their own judgment, victims start to question their own reality. They second guess themselves and their problem-solving abilities collapse. They become helpless at making decisions and are totally dependent on the abuser for guidance, which only propels them further into the abuser's reality, slipping further and further away from their own.

According to Darlene Lancer, JD, LMFT of *Psychology Today*, the effects of gaslighting are insidious the longer it occurs. In the beginning, victims don't realize they are even affected by it but slowly lose trust in their "own instincts and perceptions."[39] Victims believe their relationship has been built on trust and mutual love, which is why they are willing to believe the lies and are less likely to see they are being manipulated and controlled.

---

[39] Lancer, 2018.

Once the gaslighting effect has reached its peak, there is no reasoning with the narcissist; every thought and opinion is met with confrontation. A victim's feelings become a place of argument as they struggle desperately to gain understanding from someone incapable of sympathizing/empathizing with how they feel. They are distraught and riddled with anxiety as that high they were once on with the narcissist has slipped away, and they long for that remembrance of peace. It is like the narcissistic supply has vanished, and they begin to go through withdrawal symptoms. The reason this experience is so deadly for the victim is the imprint gaslighting leaves behind. It is not pretty; in fact, it is downright dark and ugly.

Remember, there will be no good memories made from this point on, only a world where the victim's mental and emotional torture only intensifies. Days of breaking down are followed by one good day, and the human spirit becomes crushed. Some victims cannot cry anymore because they lost the ability to feel. Zest for life slips away and is replaced by insurmountable sorrow.

These negative thoughts and images, in turn, create a host of negative emotional states such as anger, depression, anxiety, guilt, and shame. Naturally, if an individual is bogged down in bad feelings, it is difficult to do things well or engage in positive behavior. And as a result, victims may exhibit social withdrawal, avoidance, dishonesty, aggression, and even drug and alcohol abuse.

Victims start feeling on edge. They have high defense mechanisms, which creates an emotional dependency. To survive what is happening to them, the victim is in the grip of Stockholm syndrome, and these defense mechanisms act as a clever survival strategy.

Alone and isolated, the victim is reduced to a mere shadow of their former self, while the puppet master tightens the strings. Feelings that a narcissist triggers in their victims has a devastating affect over time, wearing down the victim's will and joy in life as the victim begins to lose their sense of self.

A complete system breakdown occurs as the victim continues their high defense against the gaslighting attempts. This defense is nothing when facing the narcissist's gaslighting marathon; the abuser is now accomplishing what they set out to do to their victim in the first place. The victim feels overwhelmed, confused, isolated, and depressed as they become depleted of all psychic energy and now begin to feel a loss of themselves, the self they remember they once were.

According to Robin Stern, PhD, author of the book "The Gaslight Effect: How to Spot and Survive the Hidden Manipulation Others Use to Control Your Life," victims of gaslighting often feel the following ways:

- A shell of the person they once were
- Increased anxiety and a decrease in confidence
- Self-critical and feeling overly sensitive
- Feeling to blame when things go wrong
- Always apologizing
- A feeling like something is wrong but not understanding why
- Second guessing responses
- Making excuses for the behavior of others
- Hiding new relationships from friends and family
- Feeling isolated and all alone
  Difficulty making decisions
- Feelings of hopelessness and losing enjoyment of life[40]

Eventually there comes a time when the victim has a complete shutdown and is in a gripping sense of danger. Sadly, many victims are murdered in the end. The goal for the narcissistic gaslighter is the complete annihilation of their victim, and these are the possibilities they are hoping for: suicide, psych ward, death, joyless life, no support, no friends, no money, and so on.

The narcissist wants their victim in complete misery and once they have become a liability to the narcissist, the final discard is sure to follow.

[40] Morris, Susan York. "The Gaslight Effect: How to Spot and Survive the Hidden Manipulation Others Use to Control Your Life by Robin Stern." Goodreads, 1 May 2007, www.goodreads.com/book/show/875365.The_Gaslight_Effect.

Chapter 8

Gaslighting - Final Discard

People are only used by narcissists to serve a purpose. Once that purpose has been accomplished, the person is punished for their bad behavior and dismissed in the final discard. Narcissists never get emotionally attached; therefore, they can move on with ease. It is cold, heartless, and instant, as the mask is off as the narcissist gears up to dispose of the pesky, unwanted victim.

According to Spiritual Counselor the Little Shaman, who is also a specialist in Cluster B personality disorders, narcissists may discard their victim for a few reasons:

- The victim is no longer a vital, energy supply and has been depleted, which makes them boring, weak and pathetic;

- The victim has been so destroyed they no longer give the narcissist the reactions they thrive off of;

- The narcissist has found a new rich, vital supply, someone who is typically an "upgrade." This new person cannot see they are being scammed yet. [41]

Sadly, for many victims the final discard means death. Sociopathic narcissists can snap in a violent rage and kill their victims, whereas the psychopath will kill only when necessary and they believe they can get away with it. The psychopath kills in a thought-out and planned strike; the sociopath kills while enraged. Either way, the narcissist obtains pure pleasure in killing their victim and will typically do this upon complete rejection, meaning that they no longer have possession and control and will kill out of anger. They want to make the victim pay and will obtain the instant gratification of when the victim is begging and pleading, while fighting for their life. Once the victim is dead, the thrill is gone, and some narcissists even realize they would have been better off keeping their victim alive, a regret that always falls on the tail of a prison sentence.

---

[41] Shaman, The Little. "What Happens When a Narcissist Discards You." Paired Life, 2017, pairedlife.com/problems/Discarded-by-The-Narcissist.

According to the Centers for Disease Control and Prevention (CDC), over 10 million women and men are victims of intimate partner violence in the United States each year.[42] In another study conducted by the CDC, it was found that half of all female homicide victims are killed by intimate partners.[43]

Tia Bloomer, 19 years old, was an innocent victim to a senseless, intimate murder. She was stabbed to death in front of dozens of people in Oklahoma City at bus station on March 16, 2012. Charged with the murder is Isaiah Tryon, the father of her child. Tryon had a history of violence against Bloomer, and at the time of her death, she was on her way to file a protective order against Isaiah.[44]

Like Tia Bloomer, many victims are trying to escape the abuse and get away, though sadly establishing "no contact" is always the recommended way to go, some narcissists consider this insult to an already fuming narcissistic injury and become enraged for the immediate gratification will kill in a fit of blind rage. Narcissists who murder their partners do it in an intimate, personal manner.

If not in a fit of blind rage, the narcissist will plan a more elaborate type of murders, such as:

1. Murder for Hire

Narcissists who do not want blood on their hands will craft an elaborate scheme to murder their victims in a crime in disguise by hiring someone to commit the perfect murder so they get off scot-free. Even after 30 years of marriage, there are narcissists who leave to go to work while the hit-man they hired slips through the back door, ready to carry out the crime. The narcissist is ready for a phone call from the police saying their loved one has been murdered and is ready to play the heartbroken spouse.

2) Staged Suicide

[42] "Intimate Partner Violence, Sexual Violence and Stalking." *Facts Everyone Should Know About Intimate Partner Violence, Sexual Violence and Stalking*, NISVS, 2017, www.cdc.gov/violenceprevention/pdf/NISVS-infographic-2016.pdf.
[43] Domonoske, Camila. "CDC: Half of All Female Homicide Victims Are Killed by Intimate Partners." NPR, 21 July 2017, www.npr.org/sections/thetwo-way/2017/07/21/538518569/cdc-half-of-all-female-murder-victims-are-killed-by-intimate-partners.
[44] "Death Sentence Upheld for Oklahoman in Bus Station Stabbing.", NewsOK, 31 May 2018, NewsOK.com.

Considering victims are an emotional wreck because of all the gaslighting, the narcissist may elect to murder the victim and make it look like a suicide. The police show up to the victim who has died from a single gunshot wound to the head and a suicide note beside the body. The police will rule out homicide, allowing the narcissist to get away with murder. The victim dies in vain, having been painted as unstable and crazy rather than the victim of senseless, cruel, intentional, malicious abuse.

The final discard always results in disposal – If not physically, the victim will be "murdered psychologically in death by covert abuse." [45] At this point, victims encounter the ultimate cruelty, as the narcissist has depleted them of all vital, soulful energy, leaving only a carcass behind. Since this energy is no longer present, the narcissist must search for a new, fresh supply to fill the void while removing every aspect of the discarded victim from their life, like they never existed at all.

According to article by Elinor Greenberg, Ph.D. .,"Narcissists are notorious grudge holders" [46] therefore once they are done with someone, they are done, and therefore rarely return to prior lovers, which means narcissists have a history littered with people they now hate and refuse to speak with; they would rather only fantasize of the victim suffering in their absence. They want their victim forgotten, not remembered.[47]

The narcissist, now slighted by extreme narcissistic injury they believe the victim has caused, will sit for hours, days, even weeks to come up with creative ways to destroy the already suffering victim. They want to drive their victim into deeper despair, suffering, and heartbreak and will go to great lengths to ensure this happens. The narcissist now goes completely silent and exiles the victim, while gearing up for the ultimate in revenge.

Self-proclaimed narcissist H. G. Tudor confirms this by stating that they like to keep their victims alive because this effectively allows them to further punish them by asserting superiority and gaining retribution, something not achievable when the victim is dead.[48]

---

[45] Hubs, Marc. "Psychological Murder: Death by Covert Abuse." Owlcation, 2018, owlcation.com/social-sciences/Psychological-Murder.
[46] Greenberg, Elinor. "Do Narcissists Ever Discard People Permanently?" LinkedIn: Log In or Sign Up, 2016, www.linkedin.com/pulse/do-narcissists-ever-discard-people-permanently-greenberg-phd-cgp.
[47] Greenberg, 2016.
[48] Tudor, HG. "Why the Narcissist Wants You Dead." *Knowing the Narcissist*, 9 Aug. 2017, narcsite.com/2017/08/04/why-the-narcissist-wants-you-dead/comment-page-1/.

Sometimes victims become confused. Because they have been programmed for so long to seek clarity from the narcissist, when the narcissist starts abusing in new, unsuspecting ways, victims will reach out to the narcissist in attempts to establish peace, gain understanding, and seek closure; however, there will never be any closure. Obtaining peace and clarity is the victim's desire, but the narcissist's desire is to inflict more suffering while the lethal fog of abuse continues to hover over the victim's life, even though the narcissist appears to be nowhere around.

Victims are in a hyper vulnerable state of fear and anxiety, which allows the narcissist to put into effect a new plan of action where the eternal, covert abuse begins as the victim suffers vicious blows to their finances, friendships, family, workplace, privacy and so much more. The gloves are off and the subtleties no longer exist, as the narcissist allows the victim to see just how evil they truly are. The mask has fallen and the fragmented pieces are now what will be used to murder their victim.

Narcissist HG Tudor confirms this when he states, "narcissists can essentially murder the already broken-down victim in several different ways such as character assassination, smear campaigns, silent treatment, devalue on a whole which is punishment delivered, by which superiority has been established." [49] Victims thought the whole ordeal was over, only to be surprised that the narcissist is not done yet, there is more to come, as the narcissist deploys the following abusive techniques:

The Silent Treatment

If the victim has been left alive, the final discard is always followed by the silent treatment. The abuse was bad enough, but now this. The narcissist would never leave the victim alone before, no matter how many times they were asked, and now, just like that, the narcissist has vanished and shut down all communication. This is another abusive tactic that renders victims helpless, and many will start feeling even worse, which is why they try so hard to seek closure from the narcissist. The narcissist has now gone totally silent.

HG Tudor further explains the behavior:

"We treat you as dead without the inconvenience of actually killing you. We effectively delete you when we concentrate on the new source through the new golden period. Accordingly, by ignoring you, removing you from social media postings, blocking you, not

---

[49] Tudor, 2017.

answering your messages or calls, then we have 'killed' you and this provides us with a far more satisfactory outcome." [50]

The New Supply

Long before the narcissist disposes of their victim, chances are they had a new supply all lined up ahead of time. The narcissist has been filling the new supply with tales of woe and hardship because of their crazy, unstable partner. The new supply begins to sympathize with the wounded narcissist and a new cycle of abuse begins as the narcissist simultaneously love-bombs their new supply and dehumanizes the old one. The new victim serves as a vital, rich new energy supply for the narcissist to replenish themselves after disposing of the old one.

Lindsey Ellison of The Huffington Post says that narcissists cannot maintain their disguise for too long, which is why they will seek a new supply, so they can discard the old one and start the game anew. [51]

Smear/Distort Campaigns

The narcissist knows the victim will now try and expose the abuse, so they will work extra hard to portray the victim as a liar and a storyteller. When the narcissist effectively convinces people of this, they ruin the victim's creditability when talking about the abuse influences how people view the victim.

Narcissists will use the victim's current state of hyper anxiety to paint them as a crazy, unstable, jittery mess. They tell stories of how the victim's reactions to the abuse the victim was really being an overall defective human being, prone to psychotic emotional outbursts for no reason. They continue to explain how they tried so hard to get away for so long from a stupid, horrible person who always held them back. Sadly, many people buy into these falsehoods because the always calculating narcissist has recordings to back it up. Narcissists videotape and record victims at pre-emptive times when they are provoked into emotional responses and outbursts. When they have achieved the desired response, the record button is hit and the film is later edited to exclude any trace of a set up.

---

[50] Tudor, 2017.
[51] Ellison, Lindsey. "5 Signs Your Narcissist Is Ready to Move On." *The Huffington Post*, 12 May 2015, www.huffingtonpost.com/lindsey-ellison/5-signs-your-narcissist-i_b_6858072.html.

According to Shahida Arabi, a contributor to The Huffington Post, bestselling author, and founder of Self-Care Haven, the narcissist is believable to others when they try and depict the victim as the "crazy one" because the victim is provoked into timed, emotional reactions as the narcissist then uses to show others how crazy the victim is. The truth is rarely seen as society only sees the surface of "years of abuse the victim suffered in silent terror".[52]

Flying Monkeys

Flying monkeys are people who bully on behalf of a narcissist. The narcissist weaves tall tales and partial truths mixed with lies to frame an unrecognizable version of the victim. Flying monkeys do the bidding of the narcissist, who hides behind the scenes, calling all the shots, while playing victim to any wrongdoing.

Sharie Steins, MBA, PsyD, CATC_V, describes flying monkeys as the narcissist's main allies. They act on their behalf supporting and "encouraging the delusions of victimhood."[53]

They may elect to pay or collect on favors by getting people close to the victim to watch their every move. Sadly, the ones watching and reporting back to the narcissist could inevitably be those closest to the victim, such as co-workers, friends, family, and so on.

As the bullying via the flying monkeys' mounts, so do the victim's reactions. These reactions serve as an external supply for the narcissist, who both delights and disgusts as the victim tries desperately to find ground zero after being knocked into a new dimension.

Stalking

Narcissists, at the very root, are predators. When a narcissist stalks, they watch from a distance, which in nature is referred to an "ambush

[52] Arabi, Shahida. "Why Survivors of Malignant Narcissists Don't Get the Justice They Deserve." *The Huffington Post*, 16 July 2017, www.huffingtonpost.com/entry/why-survivors-of-malignant-narcissists-dont-get-the_us_59691504e4b06a2c8edb462e.
[53] Stines, Sharie. "The Narcissist's Fan Club (Aka Flying Monkeys)." *The Recovery Expert*, 17 May 2017, pro.psychcentral.com/recovery-expert/2016/07/the-narcissists-flying-monkeys/.

predator". Ambush predators don't give chase; instead, they use cover so they can surprise unsuspecting prey.[54]

The narcissist has claimed to be finished, wanting nothing to do with the discarded victim; therefore, the victim is entitled to move on without any interference from someone who is no longer a part of their life, but the narcissist doesn't see things this way. Instead narcissists believe the victim is still their property and their desire to control them has not ended yet, therefore stalking is the perfect way for the narcissist to keep "current" in the victim's life while going undetected. Now the victim is being further violated because the narcissist has no business knowing anything about the victim's life, such as new relationships, work, friends, activities, and so on.

Hire Private Investigator

The narcissist will begin a big investigation, which requires the help of skilled professionals, such as private investigators. This is an ace in the hole for the narcissist who wants people to believe the victim is a danger to themselves and needs constant monitoring and supervision. The private investigator has no idea that they have been hired under false pretenses. The narcissist can now stalk with validation because they are not really the ones doing it. By using a private investigator, this allows the narcissist to gain information and look legit regarding how they are going about it. They claim to be investigating for the welfare of the victim when in fact, this is only a cover for their real motive, which is to violate all boundaries and personal rights of freedom the victim is entitled to.

Listening and Tracking Devices

The narcissist plants bugs in victim's private spaces such as their office, home, and car. Both audio and video devices can be strategically placed. A tracking device can always be placed underneath the car to keep track of the victim's whereabouts . This is dangerous because the narcissist could want to use these coordinates to cause harm to the victim at a specific location and time.

The bedroom, bathroom, and other personal spaces can be violated if the narcissist decides to enter the premises when they know the victim

---

[54] Martinez-Lewi, Linda. "Tag: Get out of Clutches of Narcissist." *The Narcissist in Your Life*, 2012, thenarcissistinyourlife.com/tag/get-out-of-clutches-of-narcissist/.

will not be home. The victim returns home and is now being watched in the most personal of places. The victim is moving on with life, but unbeknownst to them, they are being watched in their most intimate, private moments that no one should be able to see. This feeds the narcissist's sick, twisted obsession, as they feel like they are right there with the victim who is desperately trying to move on.

Watch the victim online

The victim's social media accounts become a way for the narcissist to keep tabs on their victim. People post innocently to their social media pages, not realizing the hidden dangers. Not only is the victim being watched by the narcissist and the flying monkeys but could be approached for a date by someone directly associated with the narcissist. This also allows the narcissist to keep up-to-date on everywhere the victim goes, their personal thoughts, people they associate with, and everything else in between.

Tap into the phone

A simple link can be sent via email and as soon as the victim clicks on it, the narcissist now has remote camera access and can watch the victim any time they are holding their phone.

As if this is not enough, the narcissist can also tap into the phone line and listen to conversations. If they are parked close enough to the cell phone signal and their device is ready, they can gain access to personal conversations.

Interrogate others

The narcissist might feel they need more answers, in which case they will try and establish communication with the victim's inner circle of people. They begin asking questions, trying to get answers, or making sure messages get delivered to the victim. This instills more fear in the already fearful victim.

Park and watch

At night when the victim has the curtains open, the curious narcissist must always keep tabs on their victim and will just sit in the car for hours watching every movement, like a predator observing their prey before they move in for the kill. The narcissist keeps the victim's timing down this way as well, making sure to know exactly what they are doing after being discarded because the sadistic narcissist wants the victim to suffer, not prosper. This allows them to see for themselves what the victim is really up to in order to gauge whether they should step up the abuse and add a little terror to the mix, so their victim won't feel so relaxed in their own home.

Taking Away Police/Legal Support

When victims react to bullying and abuse, the narcissist is just waiting to use the reactions to show the police that the victim is harassing them. Now the police are being gaslit by the narcissist who would love nothing more than to see their old victim in jail, behind bars for as long as possible. The more the victim tries to reach out, the more the narcissist is using this to display that the victim just wants them back. The narcissist uses this to draw in more people who can be used to bully the already broken victim.

When the victim tries to defend themselves, the narcissist may elect to claim harassment and turn the tables on the victim by taking all police support away. The victim is left helpless and cannot contact the police because the narcissist has convinced law enforcement they are being victimized. Narcissists love using the legal system against their victims by pulling in people in positions to cause the victim more suffering.

Framing the Victim for Murder

The narcissist would love nothing more than to see their victim behind bars for the rest of their life. If the narcissist who desires the ultimate revenge could pull this off, they have got it made. They staged a murder to look like the victim did it and now they win; their plan worked like a charm. What was the plan, you wonder? What did the narcissist do to cause their victim to be sentenced to life behind bars? Well, I will explain a scenario where this is the outcome.

In this case, there is a murder at a local convenience store. The narcissist committed the murder but placed the victim's DNA at the scene and crafted an incredible plan to make it foolproof. Several street people who are always around at certain times were paid by the narcissist to tell police and court officials that they saw the victim at the time of the murder. At the time, the narcissist knew the victim was alone at home with no creditable alibi, and after an investigation, the victim is arrested for murder and ends up getting convicted, sentenced to live in prison.

The narcissist has achieved the impossible. The victim was already abused for years prior and now the narcissist has made the victim pay and framed them for a murder they did not commit. The victim will now suffer the rest of their lives, which gives the narcissist the greatest amount of satisfaction.

Suicide

The narcissist is also trying to get the victim committed for a mental evaluation based on how crazy and unstable they are and will work extra hard trying to convince as many as possible of this, especially those closest to the victim. The more people they have successfully convinced, the greater the danger for the already-battered victim trying to emotionally debrief from the whole experience.

The victim, now turned survivor, is left with feelings of shock, disbelief, sadness, anxiety, panic attacks, guilt, shame, fear, anger, and loneliness, all while suffering with the massive loss such as children, finances, living, support, friends, family, etc. This outcome can lead many victims to suicide, feeling such deep despair and no desire to carry on.

The victim spent most of their existence living in fear and just because the narcissist is no longer around in person, that fear never subsides. This allows the same fear that was experienced during the abuse to continue while having a huge impact on the now survivor's overall health and ability to move on from the abuse.

Clinical psychologist Mr. Adedotun Ajiboye states that emotional abuse leads to severely imbedded fear because fear is one's natural response to danger, psychological abuse comes with dangerous effects such as tiredness, sleeplessness, anxiety, and depression, which sadly may lead to suicide. Also, victims can have physical complications such as heart disease, ulcers and so on. Mr Adedotun Ajiboye further claims that psychological abuse produces the ultimate in emotional trauma.[55]

The traumatized survivor now has the ultimate journey of healing ahead of them. This journey involves finding a new normal, establishing strong

---

[55] "Why Psychological Abuse Is Worse than Physical." *Vanguard News*, Vanguard, 7 May 2018, www.vanguardngr.com/2018/05/psychological-abuse-worse-physical/.

boundaries, learning to love and accept themselves, understanding they are not alone, and cycling through all the pain, emotions, and clarity that come during the healing process.

Chapter 9
The Aftermath of Abuse

The survivor made it out alive, but that is no consolation when they are left riddled with feelings of self-doubt, confusion, shock, disbelief, anxiety, depression, sadness, and pain.

While the abuse took place, memories became replaced by feelings to protect the body from the unbearable levels of fear and anxiety. These heightened feelings do not just go away after the survivor is out of the toxic environment. The abuse was so rapid that remembering every detail became replaced with an overall feeling of gloom and the details were buried.

Survivors may have a hard time recalling specific moments and verbal exchanges because the mind does not want to remember. To recall these events would be too overwhelming, so the brain shuts off the ability to remember as a form of self-preservation. In the aftermath, survivors are left cycling through immense pain, paranoia, fear, anxiety, depression, and a whole host of feelings and moods, causing further trauma. It is this reason abuse survivors have symptoms instead of memories; the root is drenched in extreme trauma.

In fact, this when the survivor may feel the worst. They are trying piece together what just happened to them while everything is still fresh, and the totality of what has taken place remains foggy. The survivor is unable to properly begin to heal because they are experiencing a heavy dose of trauma that will grow and intensify, even after the abuse is over. This type of trauma brings on a whole host of feelings and states of being. We will discuss some of these feelings below.

Shock and Confusion

The narcissist spent so much time creating a false reality that after the abuse is over, survivors have a hard time finding a new sense of normal — they have lost touch with what normal is. Their normal was an array of falsehoods created for them by someone hell-bent on destroying them. It is hard to reconcile something like that when hurting people is unimaginable to the empathetic survivor; they can't understand why someone they love would do such horrible things to them.

Overwhelming Pain and Sadness

Pain washes over survivors in waves. During these episodes, survivors find it overwhelming. They feel as if they are being suffocated, making it harder to cycle through the pain; it is as if they are caught in the flight-or-fight mode. Once a survivor understands that they must embrace pain and ride it out over the waves until they are released safely upon the shore. By embracing this process, the flow of pain begins to minimize, until eventually it dissipates altogether.

Anxiety

Anxiety is a feeling of worry or nervousness, typically about an imminent situation or an outcome with an uncertain result. Abuse can heighten these feelings of anxiety. Now that the abuse is technically over, the anxiety does not necessary stop. In fact, with many survivors, it increases.

A Florida State University study shows people who were verbally abused had 1.6 times as many symptoms of depression and anxiety as those who had not been verbally abused. They were also twice as likely to have suffered a mood or anxiety disorder over their lifetime, according to Natalie Sachs-Ericsson, a psychology professor and the study's lead author.[56]

Always on guard with gripping fear, that anxious feeling from deep within never really goes away. In fact, this is just one of the elements that linger on well after the abuse is over; survivors have basically been left a nervous wreck.

That feeling of nervousness remains as survivors are left with a heightened sense of awareness, at times appearing paranoid or delusional. Staying calm, cool, and collected is virtually impossible, and emotional episodes are far from over as the recovering survivor feels like they are short-circuiting on the inside.

Depression / Suicidal Thoughts

The trauma has been enormous, and so will be the depression to follow. Many survivors drop to an all-time low and feel as if there is no reason to carry on; they fall into a pit of despair. The pain they are experiencing is so

---

[56] "Invisible Scars: Verbal Abuse Triggers Adult Anxiety, Depression." *ScienceDaily*, 22 May 2006, www.sciencedaily.com/releases/2006/05/060522150701.htm.

deep, it virtually takes over every aspect of their life until it feels more like a constant state of misery. With fragments of hope slipping away, this is when many survivors take their lives or suffer in silence with suicidal thoughts and feelings.

According to the United States Department of Justice, domestic victimization is correlated with a higher rate of depression and suicidal behavior.[57]

Disconnect from Self and Life

Numb from the whole ordeal, survivors experience feelings of emptiness and are at a complete loss regarding who they really are. Their whole sense of normal has been turned upside down, and now they do not even know who they are. As a result, they naturally begin withdrawing from life. Most survivors remain in seclusion as they come to terms with what happened while trying to get back in touch with themselves again.

Isolation/ Lack of Support

In an abusive environment, survivors became solely dependent on their abuser to provide their very sense of reality and gradually isolate themselves from the outside world. In the aftermath of abuse, survivors may become further isolated when they cut off contact with anyone remotely associated with the narcissist, which makes things that much more difficult. There is no getting around it; their inner circle needs to be small, so they do not find themselves fending off more attacks. Because of this, survivors may feel as if they have nowhere to turn. Highly vulnerable, alone, scared, disorientated, and confused, many survivors become completely withdrawn. Some become so alone all they must depend on is themselves.

Seek Support from Abuser

During this confusing time, many survivors run back to their abusers to apologize, in hopes of gaining peace and some level of comfort. Survivors have been so accustomed to seeking validation, approval, and clarity from the narcissist that it is hard to rewire this pattern of thinking. The ever-lasting belief that the narcissist will change and see the error of their ways is a

---

[57] Truman, 2013.

juvenile hope brought on by fairy tales and happily ever after's; it is not a feeling for narcissistic abuse survivors.

According to Lindsey Ellison of The Huffington Post, a narcissistic vortex sucks victims in with no way out and constant attempts to rationalize with the narcissist, or get some kind of emotional response with no return. The survivor will never get the narcissist to change their mind or see things the victim's way. So if a survivor keeps reaching out, they will be forever stuck in a vortex and unable to move on.[58]

It is vital to understand that there will never be any closure from a narcissist because all narcissists refuse to be held accountable and will never accept being confronted for their horrible actions. The cornerstone of every narcissist is denial, and they are not about to admit to anything. This must be embraced to successfully move on and heal.

Narcissistic abuse is so surreal that you must go through it to believe it, and even then, it is still hard to believe.

As the healing begins, survivors can re-connect with their inner psyche and cycle through many thoughts, feelings and emotions such as anger, denial, pain, and despair. Now empowered with the knowledge of what has been happening, survivors may begin to build strong barriers to protect against future attacks.

Awareness is the water that will extinguish the flames of the gaslighting effect and enable survivors to move toward relying on their own judgment again. Healing is a process that opens the windows of the mind to a world of discovery; both abuse and of themselves. Now survivors need to journey back to reality and start building a new foundation of personal boundaries, self-care, self-respect, strength, fortitude, and courage. The pain gradually begins to lessen, anxiety subsides, fear loosens, depression lifts, and a glimmer of hope begins to shine through the darkness.

Sonia Connolly, author of "Wellspring of Compassion and Presence After Trauma" claims victims should listen to their instincts as they re-build self-trust and repair their broken reality by tuning into internal signals with interested curiosity[59].

[58] Ellison, Lindsey. "The #1 Trick to Engaging withA Narcissist." *The Huffington Post*, 8 Nov. 2014, www.huffingtonpost.com/lindsey-ellison/the-1-secret-on-how-to-en_b_5785616.html.
[59] Connolly, Sonia. "Welcome." Sundown Healing Arts, 1 June 2012, traumahealed.com/articles/repair-your-reality-after-gaslighting/.

Self-discovery is a fundamental component in healing, and, during this journey, many treasures hidden deep within start revealing themselves. Looking inward helps survivors understand how to make better choices in the future by only allowing positive energy to flow in and out. The love that had been suppressed for so long can now come alive now through acts of kindness and compassion on themselves, while fostering a healthy outlook on what is to come. The days of gloom and doom are over, as it is time to celebrate all the incredible milestones about to happen. A new adventure is about to begin: the road to recovery.

Chapter 10

Revealing and Healing

Now that the abuse is over, it is time for survivors to celebrate freedom and a new-found sense of self. This is when clarity starts to happen as survivors begin to recall the abuse and understand the full scope of what they experienced.

Survivors continue to heal as they begin to understand the entire picture. Acknowledging that the horrible things the narcissist did were not right and not the survivor's fault are vital to the healing process. These realizations typically come with self-reflection.

Nobody is perfect, and for too long, the narcissist has been using the survivor's flaws to paint them as a defective human being who was not worthy of existing. Now it is time to take that power back by embracing all the flaws the narcissist used against the survivor — flaws are what make people human. The narcissist's flaws — cruelty, maliciousness, games, lies, deceit, and falsehoods — are far greater than any flaws that an honest individual with true intention would have. The narcissist knew what they were doing, and the survivor was responding to the horrible treatment, which was perfectly normal under the circumstances of psychological abuse.

There have been many losses because of this toxic relationship with a narcissistic predator. Some were financial, some personal, and some related to work and reputation. By now, victims have had a chance to debrief from the whole ordeal and are beginning to establish a new sense of normal. The fog is parting, and there are glimpses of sunlight peeking through the clouds as the realization sets in.

With gaslighting, survivors felt as though the ground was always shifting beneath them. There was no center of gravity, as they were made to believe up is down, so now is time to navigate back to reality and learn to trust in one's own judgment again.

The survivor must have their wits about them, and there is no room for error. The inner circle needs to become so tight that only a few people will fit. Boundaries need to be established, and intuition should become a survivor's greatest tool as they return back to their psyche that had been destroyed for so long. Gone are the days of being a "yes" person, and now learning to say "no" more often will help protect the new boundaries. Being cautious of who is allowed in will help defer more narcissists who will try and approach the survivor, especially when they are in a vulnerable state of repair.

Abigail Brenner of *Psychology Today* suggests these seven tips to help establish healthy boundaries:

Know thyself

Get to know yourself on a personal level by learning what is comfortable, important, and valuable to you. Get back in touch with your inner self and embrace all the wonderful qualities you possess.

Take personal responsibility

Becoming self-aware allows you to take responsibility for yourself and do what needs to be done by setting boundaries. By doing this, you are establishing how others will treat you. Now it's up to you to decide who comes into your personal space and if they deserve to be there.

Develop healthy self-respect

All your past experiences shape you into who you are and now it is time to make sure no one besides you can define or control who you are ever again. When you respect yourself, you will never allow others to treat you badly again.

Heed the warning signs

Stay away from people who have their own agenda where you are concerned and think nothing of pushing the limits with you. If anyone invades your personal space for their own selfish needs, they must be cut off swiftly.

Do not try to fix people

Fixing people is a way of trying to achieve validation, attention, and love. It is important to understand narcissists cannot be fixed and are not interested in becoming any different than they already are.

Take charge of choices

You have every right to change your mind or direction at will and never owe anyone an explanation for your choices. If anyone mistreats you, do not be afraid to walk away, guilt-free and without any fear.

Separate from others

Now it is time to be emotionally attached while remaining psychologically and intellectually detached, which is the ability to separate thoughts, feelings, and beliefs from those of others. This provides space to allow for personal expression to come alive while minimizing psychological ties and all conflict.[60]

It is time to be strategically private and keep a low profile because chances are, even though the narcissist appears to be gone, they may still be lurking in the background. Perhaps they are trying to send someone in to befriend the survivor to enter their life for the sole purpose of keeping tabs. Whatever the possibilities, it is best to practice caution when meeting new people, especially now while still vulnerable. Let the experience with the narcissist serve as a valuable lesson in never allowing another person to take control like that ever again.

Time for a little self-care, self-love, and self-compassion as peace and serenity return to a life once riddled with strife, drama, and chaos. Now that the abuse is over, the body and mind have a chance to debrief from the whole experience. Survivors can now begin to heal the trauma.

Developing self-compassion is vital, which Kristin Neff, a pioneering self-compassion researcher, author, and teacher, describes as a three-step process:

1. Instead of getting angry with yourself for being stupid enough to fall for the abusive tactics, be gentle and understand the narcissist does not care about the feelings of others

2. See the experience as part of a bigger picture and realize this happens to a lot of people and in a lot of different ways. Embrace the flaws the narcissist worked so hard to exploit and realize that nobody is perfect.

3. Embrace the painful feelings without over thinking them. Be aware of feelings while keeping a healthy distance.[61]

---

[60] Brenner, Abigail. "7 Tips to Create Healthy Boundaries with Others." *Psychology Today,* Sussex Publishers, 2015, www.psychologytoday.com/ca/blog/in-flux/201511/7-tips-create-healthy-boundaries-others.
[61] Truman, 2014.

Time will open the windows to clarity as the mind relaxes and the survivor begins to connect with their spiritual energy once again. Healing after abuse is like becoming a brand-new person. A survivor of abuse sheds the silhouetted fragments of who they once were to become brand new as a new phenomenon takes places at the core, the very essence of a beautiful soul, once so very lost. Now it is time for a healthy, happy new you to emerge.

Welcoming A Happy, Healthy New You

It is your time now so let us kick it into high gear and start enjoying life again. Your time has come; you have gone through hell, and now it is time to create a little piece of heaven, right inside of you.

It took you a long time to get here, so it is only sensible that it will take some time to feel better. Be gentle with yourself as you begin your journey of self-discovery and healing. Always remember that every journey begins with a single step, a step that you are taking now. Feel proud of yourself — you deserve it!

You are learning so many valuable lessons as you journey through the healing process and the most important lesson of them all is to never be fooled again by a narcissistic predator, who's only intentions are to abuse you and feed off of your good nature.

Once Bitten, Twice Shy

You were fooled once, but you will not be fooled again and now are able to understand the difference between evil and broken.

A broken person can be fixed, however a narcissist cannot. A narcissist causes pain and suffering, while a broken person would not even contemplate because they know what it feels like to hurt. Try to never confuse someone who can be saved from someone you need to be saved from.

Keep Calm and a Low Profile

Keeping emotions in check was especially difficult during the abuse. Now that the abuse is over, there are still triggers left behind. These triggers come from lingering anxiety and previous defense mechanisms. In time, these will subside, but for now, while everything is still fresh, it is good to remember the narcissist is using all emotional reactions against you. Even now that the narcissist appears to be gone, they may still be looking to get you riled up and to provoke emotional reactions to further their ongoing campaign of victimhood. These reactions were the cornerstone to all the abuse you just traveled through, so now it is time to understand this and keep those emotions in check.

Narcissists gain the upper hand when your reactions and behavior to the abuse are so outrageous it overshadows the abuse itself. The narcissist's claim that you are crazy will only seem justified, so now you need to play along, only this time by your rules. At times, it may be difficult to control, but you must not let your former abuser ever see you sweat. Keep it all tucked in and out of the public eye. Now is the time to keep a low profile on social media. Each time you let loose with yourself, the narcissist and their cohorts are there grabbing every single screenshot to lend credibility to the narcissist's lies about you. You will be saving grace by going low-key and ultra-private even if you must become a ghost.

As the windows of your mind continue to expand and as you start to re-connect with your spirit energy, you will gain inner peace, self-control, forgiveness, and self-love. Take time to breathe and regain your serenity that has been lost for so long. It is your time to heal. Shut out the noise and bring in the silence; it is time to de-brief.

Take Care of Your Body

The emotional battering, like the depression that follows, takes a toll on your physical and emotional self. It is now time to research healthy, all-natural, well-balanced nutrition as vital nutrients need to be part of your road to recovery. This is the time to refuel by treating your body with the care that you have been starved of for too long.

Counseling for Abused

Entering counseling that is especially designed for abused individuals will help work your emotions out. Not all therapists are aware of gaslighting, so be careful who you chose. It's vital that the person you are talking to isn't only aware of gaslighting but knows how to help re-stabilize you to your own reality and better help you understand yourself.

A therapist's office is a safe place to open and start to formulate a solid for healing. The therapist will suggest many coping strategies to help you on your healing journey such as relaxation techniques, self-compassion, and self-care. Every therapist is different in their approach, so look around and make sure your therapist is someone who gives you a sense of calm. After everything you have just been through, a calm, soothing environment is precisely what you need right now.

You will be able to get everything off your chest. Allowing those feelings to come out will help you tremendously during the healing process.

Take on a Hobby

Allow a passion to grow by letting the creative juices flow. Photography, painting, writing, and poetry are just some ideas to allow the mind to play, and the inner child to come alive. Chances are it's been awhile since you felt relaxed enough to enjoy life and pursue a passion. Now is the time to stimulate your senses.

Support System

It is time to be careful of your inner circle and start removing those that do not belong there. Continue to be cautious of who you allow in. Keep only those who have no association to the narcissist but try not to isolate yourself. Reach out to those who have had similar experiences and support one another. Be careful what you tell people and remember that not everyone can be trusted. It is known that even the closest people can be the most lethal ones who stab you in the back.

Take Time with God

God has been there all along as you held on to faith, barely hanging on to hope, but you did it. Everything happens in God's timing because God will not allow you to see what you are not ready for. As you form a strong spiritual connection, it is important to pray and seek guidance with God. May it be your mantra to always be thankful to God. Be thankful you made it through and understand that your experience may be used to suit a higher purpose. Maybe you will use this to educate others, you just never know, but guess who does? God does.

God will show you the error of your own ways as well; after all, we are responsible in life for our choices, and God wants us to recognize this. During the healing and revealing process, God has many treasures that await you on the other side of abuse.

Rejuvenation

All these beautiful treasures deep within you may now become awakened again after a long period of oppression. Gone are the days when you were gripped with fear and anxiety because the new you are becoming so much stronger, wiser, and better with each passing day. You are learning so many new things about yourself and how unique and precious you really are, all contrary to how the narcissist made you feel about yourself.

You now realize just how valuable you are and that all those things once criticized by a cruel narcissist are what makes you uniquely special. Those who absolutely love you will accept you for who you are. You are learning to embrace your flaws, and nobody will ever be able to use them against you.

The light of love is now shining again. You are laughing, smiling, and enjoying the simple things in life. This is your time to shine. May your light of love never be dimmed again.

Abuse is Serious

Narcissists are dangerous people and not to be taken lightly. Their intentions will always be cruel. Once the abuse switch has been flipped, the abuse picks up speed and momentum, like a train barreling down the track, relentlessly out of control, headed for a final impact, which unfortunately leads to death for some. The U.S. Department of Justice reports that intimate partner violence accounts for 15 percent of all violent crime.[62]

Abuse does not magically stop. Couples counseling should not be considered an option when dealing with dangerous abuse because the perpetrator (narcissist) manipulates the therapists just as they do everyone else around them. Narcissists all operate with a similar pattern of cruelty and love to fool people. Do not let them make a fool out of you by tuning them in. Narcissists want to instill fear in the victim and those closest to them, and this is how they maintain their power. Strip them of their power by reporting the abuse and getting yourself or loved ones to safety immediately!

The National Coalition Against Domestic Violence (NCADV) reports that one in three women and one in four men have been victims of [some form of] physical violence by an intimate partner within their lifetime.[63]

---

[62] USDOJ, 2014.
[63] Black, 2010.

Victims often fail to accept the danger because they have become helplessly trauma-bonded to their abuser. All rational thinking and reasoning are not present, so someone else needs to step in. Never hesitate to help someone who is being abused and/or second-guess whether you are making the right decision or not. If you are protecting someone's life, it will always be the right decision.

On average, nearly 20 people per minute are physically abused by an intimate partner in the United States. For one year, this equates to more than 10 million women and men.[64] Victims of abuse are in constant danger, so do not delay. Act right away! If you or someone you know is in an abusive situation, please visit the websites below or call the hotlines for further assistance.

United States

Shelters: www.domesticshelters.org
Abuse Hotline: www.thehotline.org

Canada

Shelters: www.sheltersafe.ca
Abuse Hotline: www.endingviolencecanada.org

England

Shelters: https://www.doorway.org.uk
Abuse Hotline: https://www.victimsupport.org.uk

Australia

Shelters: https://www.womenscommunityshelters.org.au/
Abuse Hotline: https://thesamaritans.org.au/

---

[64] Black, 2010.

Works Cited

Ambardar , Sheenie. "Diagnostic and Statistical Manual of Mental Disorders (DSM–5)." *DSM-5*, 2018, www.psychiatry.org/psychiatrists/practice/dsm.

Ambardar, Sheenie. "What are the DSM-5 Diagnostic Criteria for Narcissistic Personality Disorder (NPD)?" *Latest Medical News, Clinical Trials, Guidelines – Today on Medscape*, 16 July 2018, www.medscape.com/answers/1519417-101773/what-are-the-dsm-5-diagnostic-criteria-for-narcissistic-personality-disorder-npd.

Arabi, Shahida. "20 Diversion Tactics Highly Manipulative Narcissists, Sociopaths and Psychopaths Use To Silence You." *Thought Catalog*, 5 Oct. 2018, thoughtcatalog.com/shahida-arabi/2016/06/20-diversion-tactics-highly-manipulative-narcissists-sociopaths-and-psychopaths-use-to-silence-you/10/.

Arabi, Shahida. "Why Survivors of Malignant Narcissists Don't Get the Justice They Deserve." *The Huffington Post*, TheHuffingtonPost.com, 16 July 2017, www.huffingtonpost.com/entry/why-survivors-of-malignant-narcissists-dont-get-the_us_59691504e4b06a2c8edb462e.

Begg, Ian Maynard. "Dissociation of Processes of Belief; Source Recollection, Statement Familiarity, and the Illusion of Truth." *Download Limit Exceeded*, 1992, citeseerx.ist.psu.edu/viewdoc/download?doi=10.1.1.220.6486&rep=repl&type=pdf

Black, Michele C. "National Intimate Partner and Sexual Violence Survey." *National Intimate Partner and Sexual Violence Survey Summary Report*, 2010, www.cdc.gov/violenceprevention/pdf/nisvs_report2010-a.pdf.

Black, Michele C. "National Intimate Partner and Sexual Violence Survey." *NISVS*, 2011, www.cdc.gov/violenceprevention/pdf/nisvs_report2010-a.pdf.

Bonchay, Bree. "The 4 Most Common Narc-Sadistic Triangulation Tactics." *Free from Toxic*, 25 Feb. 2018, www.freefromtoxic.com/2015/05/13/the-4-most-common-narc-sadistic-triangulation-tactics/.

Bonn, Scott A. "The Differences Between Psychopaths and Sociopaths." *Psychology Today*, Sussex Publishers, 2018, www.psychologytoday.com/us/blog/wicked-deeds/201801/how-tell-psychopath-sociopath.

Brenner, Abigail. "7 Tips to Create Healthy Boundaries with Others." *Psychology Today*, Sussex Publishers, 2015, www.psychologytoday.com/ca/blog/in-flux/201511/7-tips-create-healthy-boundaries-others.

Carver, Joseph M. "The "Small Kindness" Perception." *Love and Stockholm Syndrome*, 2016, drjoecarver.makeswebsites.com/clients/49355/File/love_and_stockhol m_syndrome.html.

Connolly, Sonia. "Welcome." *Sundown Healing Arts*, 1 June 2012, traumahealed.com/articles/repair-your-reality-after-gaslighting/.

DeFife, Jared. "DSM-V Offers New Criteria for Personality Disorders." *Psychology Today*, Sussex Publishers, 2010, www.psychologytoday.com/us/blog/the-shrink-tank/201002/dsm-v-offers-new-criteria-personality-disorders.

"Death Sentence Upheld for Oklahoman in Bus Station Stabbing.", *NewsOK*, 31 May 2018, NewsOK.com.

Descilo, Teresa. "UNDERSTANDING AND TREATING TRAUMATIC BONDS." *Trauma Therapy Articles: Descilo: Understanding and Treating Traumatic Bonds*, 2009, www.healing-arts.org/healing_trauma_therapy/traumabonding-traumaticbonds.htm.

Domonoske, Camila. "CDC: Half of All Female Homicide Victims Are Killed By Intimate Partners." *NPR*, NPR, 21 July 2017, www.npr.org/sections/thetwo-way/2017/07/21/538518569/cdc-half-of-all-female-murder-victims-are-killed-by-intimate-partners.

Ellison, Lindsey. "The #1 Trick to Engaging with A Narcissist." *The Huffington Post*, TheHuffingtonPost.com, 8 Nov. 2014, www.huffingtonpost.com/lindsey-ellison/the-1-secret-on-how-to-en_b_5785616.html.

Ellison, Lindsey. "5 Signs Your Narcissist Is Ready to Move On." *The Huffington Post*, TheHuffingtonPost.com, 12 May 2015, www.huffingtonpost.com/lindsey-ellison/5-signs-your-narcissist-i_b_6858072.html.

"Empathy | Definition of Empathy in English by Oxford Dictionaries." *Oxford Dictionaries | English*, Oxford Dictionaries, 2014, en.oxforddictionaries.com/definition/empathy.

Fallon, James. "How I Discovered I Have the Brain of a Psychopath | James Fallon." *The Guardian*, Guardian News and Media, 2 June 2014, www.theguardian.com/commentisfree/2014/jun/03/how-i-discovered-i-have-the-brain-of-a-psychopath.

"Patty Hearst." *FBI*, FBI, 18 May 2016, www.fbi.gov/history/famous-cases/patty-hearst.

Greenberg, Elinor. "Do Narcissists Ever Discard People Permanently?" *LinkedIn: Log In or Sign Up*, 2016, www.linkedin.com/pulse/do-narcissists-ever-discard-people-permanently-greenberg-phd-cgp.

Hubs, Marc. "Psychological Murder: Death by Covert Abuse." *Owlcation*, 2018, owlcation.com/social-sciences/Psychological-Murder.

"Intimate Partner Violence, Sexual Violence and Stalking." *Facts Everyone Should Know About Intimate Partner Violence, Sexual Violence and Stalking*, NISVS, 2017, www.cdc.gov/violenceprevention/pdf/NISVS-infographic-2016.pdf.

"Invisible Scars: Verbal Abuse Triggers Adult Anxiety, Depression." *ScienceDaily*, ScienceDaily, 22 May 2006, www.sciencedaily.com/releases/2006/05/060522150701.htm.

Lambert, Laura. "Stockholm Syndrome." *Encyclopædia Britannica*, Encyclopædia Britannica, Inc., 27 Apr. 2018, www.britannica.com/science/Stockholm-syndrome.

Lancer, Darlene. "How to Know If You're a Victim of Gaslighting." *Psychology Today*, Sussex Publishers, 2018, www.psychologytoday.com/ca/blog/toxic-relationships/201801/how-know-if-youre-victim-gaslighting.

Luna, Aletheia, et al. "Dear Empaths: 4 Types of Narcissists You May Be Attracting LonerWolf." *LonerWolf*, 1 Oct. 2018, lonerwolf.com/empaths-and-narcissists/.

Martinez-Lewi, Linda. "Tag: Get out of Clutches of Narcissist." *The Narcissist In Your Life*, 2012, thenarcissistinyourlife.com/tag/get-out-of-clutches-of-narcissist/.

Morris, Susan York. "The Gaslight Effect: How to Spot and Survive the Hidden Manipulation Others Use to Control Your Life by Robin Stern." *Goodreads*, Goodreads, 1 May 2007, www.goodreads.com/book/show/875365.The_Gaslight_Effect.

"Narcissistic Personality Disorder." *Psychology Today*, Sussex Publishers, 2018, www.psychologytoday.com/us/conditions/narcissistic-personality-disorder.

Ni, Preston. "6 Common Traits of Narcissists and Gaslighters." *Psychology Today*, Sussex Publishers, 2017, www.psychologytoday.com/ca/blog/communication-success/201707/6-common-traits-narcissists-and-gaslighters.

"Nonfatal Domestic Violence 2003-2012." *Bureau of Justice Statistics*, U.S. Department of Justice, 2014, www.bjs.gov/content/pub/pdf/ndv0312.pdf.

Sarkis, Stephanie A. "11 Warning Signs of Gaslighting." *Psychology Today*, Sussex Publishers, 2017, www.psychologytoday.com/us/blog/here-there-and-everywhere/201701/11-warning-signs-gaslighting.

Sarkis, Stephanie A. "Why Gaslighters Accuse You of Gaslighting." *Psychology Today*, Sussex Publishers, 2017, www.psychologytoday.com/ca/blog/here-there-and-everywhere/201702/why-gaslighters-accuse-you-gaslighting.

Shaman, The Little. "What Happens When a Narcissist Discards You." *PairedLife*, 2017, pairedlife.com/problems/Discarded-by-The-Narcissist.

Siegel, Nathan. "You Can Be Persuaded To Confess To An Invented Crime, Study Finds." *NPR*, NPR, 30 Jan. 2015, www.npr.org/2015/01/29/382483367/you-can-be-convinced-to-confess-to-an-invented-crime-study-finds.

Sol, Mateo. "Twin Flame: Your Guide to Experiencing Rare Transcendental Love " *LonerWolf*, 10 Oct. 2018, lonerwolf.com/twin-flame/.

Stines, Sharie. "The Narcissist's Fan Club (Aka Flying Monkeys)." *The Recovery Expert*, 17 May 2017, pro.psychcentral.com/recovery-expert/2016/07/the-narcissists-flying-monkeys/.

Sutton, Debra. "Sins of the Empath : Truth Seeker by Narcissist H.G. Tudor ." *Signs of a Gay Husband by Debra Sutton*, 1 Oct. 2017, signsofagayhusbandbydebrasutton.wordpress.com/2017/10/01/sins-of-the-empath-truth-seeker-by-narcissist-h-g-tudor/comment-page-1/#comment-2223.

Truman, Jennifer I. "Why Recovering from the Narcissist in Your Life Is So Hard." *Psychology Today*, Sussex Publishers, 2014, www.psychologytoday.com/intl/blog/tech-support/201606/why-recovering-the-narcissist-in-your-life-is-so-hard.

Truman, Jennifer L. "Nonfatal Domestic Violence 2003-2012." *Bureau of Justice Statistics,* US Department of Justice, 2013, www.bjs.gov/content/pub/pdf/ndv0312.pdf.

Tudor, HG. "The Super Empath." *Knowing the Narcissist*, 22 May 2018, narcsite.com/2018/05/23/the-super-empath-8/comment-page-1/.

Tudor, HG. "Why the Narcissist Wants You Dead." *Knowing the Narcissist*, 9 Aug. 2017, narcsite.com/2017/08/04/why-the-narcissist-wants-you-dead/comment-page-1/.

"Why Psychological Abuse Is Worse than Physical." *Vanguard News*, Vanguard, 7 May 2018, www.vanguardngr.com/2018/05/psychological-abuse-worse-physical/.

Westcott, Kathryn. "Hope for the Children of the Cellar." *BBC News*, BBC, 28 Apr. 2008, news.bbc.co.uk/2/hi/europe/7370889.stm.

Whitbourne, Susan Krauss. "Shedding Light on Psychology's Dark Triad." *Psychology Today*, Sussex Publishers, 2013, www.psychologytoday.com/ca/blog/fulfillment-any-age/201301/shedding-light-psychology-s-dark-triad.

Wilkinson, Alissa. "What Is Gaslighting? The 1944 Film Gaslight Is the Best Explainer." *Vox*, Vox, 21 Jan. 2017, www.vox.com/culture/2017/1/21/14315372/what-is-gaslighting-gaslight-movie-ingrid-bergman.

Index

Printed in Great Britain
by Amazon

23625851R00051